SISTERS GET THEIR KICKS
on
Route 66

Karen West and Susan Ford-West

Happy Trails

Karen West

Susan Ford-West

ISBN: 978-1-59152-164-8

Published by RJW Publishing

Text: © 2015 by Karen West and Susan Ford-West

Photography © 2015 by Karen West

For more information, write
drmorningglory@yahoo.com or
www.karenewestphotography.com

You may order extra copies of this book by calling RJW Publishing at (816) 753-7726;
or Farcountry Press toll free at (800) 821-3874.

sweetgrassbooks
an imprint of Farcountry Press

Produced by Sweetgrass Books.
PO Box 5630, Helena, MT 59604; (800) 821-3874; www.sweetgrassbooks.com.

Produced in the United States of America.

Printed in China.

19   18   17   16   15   1   2   3   4   5

Dedication

THIS IS A BOOK ABOUT WOMEN CREATING AN EPIC AND HISTORIC ADVENTURE ON ROUTE 66.
It is dedicated to the memory of a woman, our mother . . . amazing Mazie.

Two spirited "girls" who learned to love the world and adventure from their parents, but especially from their mom Mazie, created Sisters on the Fly. Mazie was the free spirit. She would try anything, and do it with style and joy. The purpose of Sisters on the Fly is to reintroduce women back to the outdoors and away from their current lives. The only rules: No men, no kids, no pets, and be nice.

We want to play like children, laugh until our tummies hurt, wear silly clothing, and share in new adventures with fellow Sisters. Route 66 was on Mazie's bucket list. We had to do it without her, but we celebrated her encouragement.

Mazie often wore costumes that delighted the Sisterhood, from red cowgirl boots to red tutus with a red boa wrapped around her neck. She was an avid fly fisher and a connoisseur of martinis and the art of smoking a cigar. She never met a stranger and was game for anything new. The Sisters treasured her and spent many hours sitting at her side, sharing a glass of wine and talking about their lives. She adored staying in our trailers and spent time reading the maps on our wandering journeys, camping around the United States, and just meeting the fine and wonderfully spirited Sisters on the Fly. Mazie was a joy to her world and ours.

She left us one day short of her ninety-fifth birthday, but we lifted our wine glasses to her and her new unknown adventure. We miss her very much. Please enjoy this book and smile when you think about the power of women. We can because we are women!

Thank you for this awesome journal: *Sisters Get Their Kicks on Route 66.*

—Maurrie and Becky

Acknowledgments

It takes a village to birth a book. There have been a plethora of midwives who attended to the process and deserve our heartfelt gratitude:

Mazie, Maurrie, Becky, and all the Sisters on the Fly who gifted us with a community of Sisters, with whom we travel, celebrate, play, dance, dress up, and learn to be girls again.

Kris, Glenda, and all the hostesses and their assistants planned for months (in excess of a year) an over-the-top twenty-five-day event that has gone down in the Sisters on the Fly history book as the largest gathering of Sisters—300-plus.

The Sisters on the Fly who participated in the Route 66 adventure: the "All the Way" Sisters, with whom we had the privilege of spending twenty-five transformative days on the road as well as all the Sisters who joined the journey for a few stops or just a few hours. Your presence enriched the collective journey and story shared in these pages. Your openness and trust made this possible.

The Route 66 Associations in all eight States traversed by the Mother Road, for preserving this piece of Americana for us and the future generations.

The Village of Pentwater, Michigan provided a lovely environment in which to birth this photo journal. Shared Space Studio shared their space with us for the third and most important summer. The Pentwater Township Library was our second home, especially the private conference room (and the twenty-four-hour Wi-Fi). The Village Grounds Coffee House provided the best espresso shots and Wi-Fi early in the morning—along with delightful employees who were interested in how the book was coming along.

Kathy Springmeyer, Director of Publications at Farcountry Press believed in this project from the very beginning and saw us through to the end. Kathy and her amazingly talented staff, Catherine Courtenaye, Ann Seifert, and Shirley Machonis took our pictures and words and created this beautiful and captivating book.

Finally, Butch our sixteen-month-old toy poodle learned how to entertain himself and sleep in the trailer a little more, and played outside with his Auntie's Cedar and Doreen while we were working. And Maggie sacrificed her Zen lifestyle to welcome into her home and heart the rambunctious personality of Butch for thirty-four days while we were gettin' our kicks on Route 66.

A special thank you to everyone who contributed to the Indigogo campaign to help get this book to print, especially Pelofsky and Associates for the generous contribution of $1,000.

Preface

From May 12 to June 5, 2015, the Sisters on the Fly (SOTF), the largest outdoor women's group in the country, undertook an epic and historic journey on America's Mother Road. Forty-nine Sisters gathered in Chicago to begin the journey. We caravanned across the country, growing in number as we traveled west to the final celebration with 269 Sisters in Ventura, California. Along the way, over 300 Sisters participated in the trip.

While this book includes pictures and information about Route 66 and the many iconic sites along the way, this is not your typical Mother Road travel guide. *Sisters Get Their Kicks on Route 66* tells the tale of a twenty-five-day trip through photos and stories of the adventures, celebrations, and Sisterhood of the women who joined the escapade.

When we first heard that SOTF was planning a Route 66 trip, we immediately knew we would do the entire trip from Chicago to Santa Monica. We decided to photograph the journey and create this book to tell the story of this amazing group of women. Ten percent of the proceeds from the sales of the book will be contributed to support outdoor education for women and children and breast cancer recovery through the Mazie Morrison Foundation, established to honor Sister #0, Mazie Morrison, the proud mother of SOTF founders, Maurrie Sussman and Becky Clarke.

We published the book to share everything wonderful that we love about SOTF with everyone who opens it. We also tried to give a small picture of the heritage and nostalgic memories of past decades of Americana preserved on Route 66.

Karen took over 8,500 images on the trip. In many ways, ours was a voyage filled with chasing or following the caravans to get in the right spots for the best shot. It was the most fun we've ever had.

From the beginning, we knew the book would be a collective endeavor. Several Sisters contributed pictures to fill in some blanks. We compiled Facebook posts and personal stories of the thirty "All the Way" Sisters to weave image, story, and fact into a unique look at a trip on the Mother Road. We hope you can hear the magic of laughter, music, and love in these pages.

—Karen West and Susan Ford-West

Happy Trails

Introduction

Come travel with the Sisters on the Fly on an adventure of epic proportions as we travel the Mother Road—famous Route 66. Through stories and photographs, this book will delight you from start to finish.

Sisters on the Fly are women who love adventure and are willing to take chances and step outside the box to seek something many would not attempt. Most have raised families and had careers ranging from attorney to homemaker, truck driver to teacher, and everything in between. Our mottos say it best: "We have more fun than anyone" and "We make Girls out of Women."

This amazing undertaking began in Joliet, Illinois, with forty-nine Sisters and their vintage trailers and ended in Santa Monica, California, with 269 Sisters. The adventure was 2,448 miles in all! Between stops there were rodeos, bag lunches, and two parades. There were catered barbecues, wading pools, limo rides to the Big Texan, ghost towns, drive-in theaters, and a police escort through Winslow, Arizona. Many found the biggest rocking chair, catsup bottle, totem pole, and pop bottle. Some Sisters went on hot air balloon rides, rafted down a river, withstood tornado warnings, and saw Clydesdale horses in the campground one morning. They stopped at as many Route 66 sights as possible. Many danced their hearts out to some of the best shit-kicking, stomp-your-feet music late into the night, and an In-N-Out Burger truck came to the last stop and grilled up 330 burgers.

The "All the Way" gals, as they are fondly referred to, those making the entire trip from start to finish, had a unique perspective on this adventure. Together for twenty-five days through hail storms, tornados, floods, and 100-plus temperatures, they formed a Sisterhood—supporting each other during emergencies great or small—made lifelong friendships, and were changed by the experience.

There is something for almost everyone here: from the participants who went all the way, to the ones who went on only a few stops, to the armchair adventurers who followed along as the Sisters traveled Route 66. Now you can join in and share the memories of days gone by through pictures and stories in this phenomenal photo journal. Approximately 300-plus Sisters and their trailers participated somewhere between Stops #1 and #14 on Route 66. So join the fun, admire the photos, and dream back to the days of traveling on the Mother Road. Enjoy the adventure.

—Kris Brown, Sister #474
SOTF National Wrangler & Route 66 Coordinator

Chicago & Joliet

PHOTO COURTESY OF RHONDA GELSTEIN

Forty-nine Sisters on the Fly gathered at the Leisure Lake Membership Resort in Joliet, Illinois, on May 12, 2015, to begin the Route 66 adventure. Among the forty-nine were thirty-one Sisters who planned on going "all the way," from Chicago to Santa Monica. Others had joined the trip for a few stops, and the local Sisters joined the fun to help our fabulous hostess, Rhonda Gelstein, Sister #2301.

"The local Sisters that pitched in and helped me with putting the event together touched me. I cherish their friendship. It was such a blessing meeting everyone, from all walks of life. I love that it doesn't matter where we come from; it's where we're going, together, that is important."
—RHONDA GELSTEIN, SISTER #2301

PHOTO COURTESY OF RHONDA GELSTEIN

It was a fine time to meet up with old friends and to make new friends who would last a lifetime.

Sharon Lambert, Sister #508, brought a map of Route 66 for the "All the Way" Sisters to sign, and we procured a large US map for each Sister to pin her home location on. This map traveled with us across the country and by the end of the trip was filled with pins from throughout the United States, with representatives from Australia and Canada too.

The next morning we boarded a charter bus and headed to Chicago and the beginning of America's Main Street—Route 66. The actual start of Route 66 has moved three times since its

ILLINOIS

Lisa Mora

SISTER #2348

I am the editor of *Vintage Caravan Magazine*. I joined the Sisters in 2011 just after I started the magazine because I was so thrilled to learn about this group of strong, independent women caravaners like me! I was the first person in Australia to join, and this trip is my first SOTF trip. I have done Route 66 before, but my dream was to do it in an old car and vintage trailer. So now I'm doing it in my 1953 Hudson Hornet towing a 15-foot 1956 Mercury and having the time of my life!

FROM LISA'S FACEBOOK PAGE:

"Hey gals, just a heads up: if you want some really awesome, classic Route 66 entertainment on the way out tomorrow, make sure you pop in and see Harley at redneck central—aka the Sandhills Curiosity Shop (it was also featured in the Cars movie) in Erick, Oklahoma. Harley's beautiful wife, Annabelle, sadly passed away last year, but these two are some of the true icons of Route 66 and they used to put on a great show including the most hilarious rendition of 'Get Your Kicks on Route 66' you will ever hear. Harley has been following our journey and would love us to stop in and say hi and let him entertain us. Make sure you detour off the highway and get some photos of his awesome store! The address is 201 South Sheb Wooley Avenue, Erick, OK 73645."

"Thank you so much Sisters, for your kind words of encouragement. I'm feeling good today. Yesterday I caught up on all my work, had my nails done, and even had an afternoon nap! What a luxury! I had an awesome camp neighbor, Dorian, who is walking the entire Route 66, resting his weary feet on his #hikeforhumanity, and he has been great company and an inspiring human. Today is going to be a great day. Dorian is back on his walk, and Doc will be coming back to me today. If you've seen the movie Cars, you'll know why I chose Doc Hudson to make this journey with me. He may be a lot older than all of your cars, but he's still a champion race car at heart, and I know he'll have me back with my Sisters in no time!"

beginning in 1933 due to the many urban developments in Chicago. The Sisters on the Fly Route 66 adventure began at the current Chicago location that marks the beginning of the Mother Road at Michigan Avenue and Adams Street.

After gathering at the "Begin Route 66" sign, the Sisters spread out to see the sights around the Windy City. A major destination was Lou Mitchell's Restaurant. Route 66 once originally began on Jackson Boulevard, and Lou Mitchell's was a favorite diner stop for travelers on the Mother Road. It seemed a logical place for breakfast.

PHOTO COURTESY OF RHONDA GELSTEIN

PHOTO COURTESY OF CINDI MLADENKA

ILLINOIS

PHOTO COURTESY OF CONNIE ANDERSON

PHOTO COURTESY OF GLENDA "G" STONE

NAVY PIER, CHICAGO

PHOTO COURTESY OF CONNIE ANDERSON

Others visited the Chicago Art Institute, directly across the street from the Route 66 sign; several went to the Navy Pier for a ride on the Ferris wheel; and a few took the major bus tour of the city.

On our last evening in Joliet, Rhonda and her team planned a wonderful kick-off celebration dinner at the Joliet Area Historical Museum and Route 66 Welcome Center, located at the true Crossroads of America where the historic Route 66 once intersected the Lincoln Highway.

Navy Pier
Chicago, IL

PHOTO COURTESY OF CONNIE ANDERSON

ILLINOIS

Ellen Franks
SISTER #548

I love to cook and create new dishes—anything to do with food! At a cooking class I met Sister #334, Laura Anderson, and although I didn't know it at the time, I was in for the ride of my life. Before I knew it I was Sister #548, pulling a trailer out of a field in Indiana and hauling it home. Laura is the reason I am a member of Sisters on the Fly. I named my trailer the Dreamcycle (rhymes with bicycle) because her theme started out being about ice cream. She represents the dream that I can still do things that are difficult, and I can have adventures.

I remember driving Route 66 as a child, hearing stories about it from my dad and grandfather, and, of course, in school. My father gave me the gift of adventure and wonder. My mother gave me independence.

I told Laura that if I did this I had to go all the way from Chicago to Santa Monica! So the trip was on. The challenge became getting time off, getting the Dreamcycle travel ready, finding a sitter for the dogs, painting, cleaning, packing, and having a backup plan.

I pulled the Dreamcycle down Lakeshore Drive to the corner of Michigan Avenue and Adams Street where the current "Begin Route 66" sign is. I followed my maps and led my little caravan on the old road each day. I found that the maps and signs are a little out of date, as more of the old route is missing and now impassable. We hit dirt roads and dead ends that we were able to laugh about and that made for great stories at the end of the day.

The last day in my caravan, the Sisters were determined to go different ways, so that was the first day I was truly on my own. With no one else to take pictures, I fumbled with a couple of shots through the windshield. When I arrived at the Ventura Fairgrounds, I was the last one through the gate. I was elated that I had finished what I started. Route 66 was a goal I had set for myself and I did it—start to finish!

"We had a table full of door prizes, and then we also gave away all of the tablescape items. Everyone went home with new Route 66-themed items. The kickoff party was held at the Joliet Historical Museum. Everyone could tour the museum as part of the event."—RHONDA GELSTEIN, SISTER #2301

The "All the Way" Sisters gathered on the steps of the museum for a special picture before we began our journey to Santa Monica.

On the morning of May 14, the Sisters hitched up and headed down the road for Litchfield, Illinois.

Springfield
& Litchfield

The caravan said goodbye to Joliet on the morning of May 14 and traveled the 208 miles to Stop #2—Springfield/Litchfield, Illinois. On the way, we made several stops and managed to stay on the Mother Road most of the way.

The first major stop was Dwight, Illinois, home to Ambler's Texaco Station, part of the National Park Service Route 66 Corridor Preservation Program. When the Sisters arrived, we made quite a scene as we attempted to park around the small, cottage-like station.

ILLINOIS

Across the street from the Texaco Station was the Old 66 Family Restaurant, where a few Sisters couldn't resist following "the Mother Road to Great Food" as we drove and ate our way across the country.

Next stop on the road was O'Dell, Illinois, home to Miller's Standard Oil Company. Built in 1932, this National Park Service preservation site has been maintained in its original condition. Again, the Sisters gathered and parked wherever they could. The little city of O'Dell has never seen such a sight and welcomed us with typical midwestern hospitality.

ILLINOIS

Melody Reed
SISTER ON THE TRY

I've had a nostalgic love for Route 66 ever since my family moved from Philadelphia, Pennsylvania, to Van Nuys, California, when I was nine years old. I don't recall a lot about that cross-country trip, but I know we spent time on Route 66 on the 3,000-plus-mile journey.

What I remember most on that journey in the 1950s are the miles and miles of two-lane highways with a lot of dips in the road. My siblings and I loved those dips, when we would lose our stomachs plunging down and rising upward with each dip. The waxed hood of our car reflected the blazing sun. We stopped at little cafes and felt like we were in another world. I decided then that I wanted to live in the beautiful state of Colorado, and here I am today!

I had just returned from a wonderful month-long trip to China to learn that my BFF, Nancy Johnston, had joined Sisters on the Fly and signed up for the Route 66 trip. She planned to take her 1971 Cardinal camper with her Ford 250 diesel truck, and she invited me to attend as a Sister on the Try! Of course, we wanted to experience as much of Route 66 as possible and were determined to go "all the way." Nothing else would do!

The weather was messy the first third of the trip, with heavy rains and hail. At times we even questioned whether or not the trip was worth it. We persevered, though, and had a great time. The kickoff in Joliet, Illinois, was wonderful.

Standing in front of the sign marking the beginning of Route 66 in Chicago, Illinois, was magical. I made a brief one-day departure to fly back to Denver to attend my grandson's high school graduation, and came back to the pouring rains of Oklahoma City! I was happy to be back on the road again. Amarillo, Texas, marked the start of sunny weather. New Mexico was "enchanting," and Arizona, especially Williams, was absolutely wonderful thanks to the mayor! The final leg of the trip to Santa Monica/Ventura, California,

was a mixture of elation and sadness—the journey was ending, but we made it "all the way"! Standing in front of the "End of Route 66" trail sign in Santa Monica was also magical.

I checked off one of my bucket list items with this trip. I met so many wonderful, strong, and independent women from all over the United States as well as Australia and Canada. There are many states supporting the Route 66 legend, moments in history that live on. America is truly a wonderful country with a rich and unique history. I'm glad that I got to go "all the way"!

Pontiac, Illinois, is all about preserving its Route 66 heritage. It's home to the Illinois Route 66 Association Hall of Fame & Museum. The Sisters loved viewing the images, stories, and history of the Mother Road. A volunteer docent opened Bob Walmire's infamous school bus for a private tour—it was the highlight of the visit.

Pontiac is also known for its murals. Twenty were created in four days during the "Walldog Summer Bash" in 2009.

The state capital is Springfield, Illinois, and Route 66 runs through it with Litchfield just a few miles to the south. A few travelers stopped in Springfield on the way to the campground and others made their way back north for a visit the next day. The home of Abraham Lincoln is a major destination in Springfield for Route 66 visitors.

Finally, after a full day of Route 66 nostalgia, forty-four of us arrived at Stop #2—Kamper Kompanion

ILLINOIS

"Who knew karaoke could be so much fun!"
—SHARON LAMBERT, SISTER #508

PHOTO COURTESY OF CONNIE ANDERSON

RV Park in Litchfield, Illinois. SOTF hostess Cyndi Kinder, Sister #3234 greeted us as we arrived, with plenty of information about the Mother Road highlights in the Litchfield/Springfield area.

We entertained ourselves with a night of karaoke and a hot dog roast. It was great fun as the Sisters sang, ate, drank, and did what we do best: have more fun than anyone!

Three miles of Route 66 run through Litchfield, and the Sisters enjoyed each mile and the historic sites. The Litchfield Museum and Route 66 Welcome Center is filled with memorabilia about the historical significance of Route 66 to the economic development of the town. The Ariston Cafe is believed to be the oldest Route 66 restaurant still operating in Illinois, and many of the Sisters descended

ILLINOIS

on it for a hearty meal. Litchfield also boasts the longest-operating drive-in movie theater on the Mother Road—the Sky View Drive-In. For coffee lovers, the Latte Litchfield Espresso Bar and Creamery was a delightful stop on the way out of town as we headed off for Stop #3—St. Louis, Missouri.

ILLINOIS

Nancy Johnston

SISTER #5445

I got my trailer last year and began the evolutionary process of creating my Cardinal Caliente. I had heard about SOTF, and when I checked the website and realized the trip was only a month away, it became #1 on my bucket list. It would be my first trip with the Sisters, and going "all the way" was the only option. I loved it!

In 1980 I was a single mom with two daughters, moving from Casper, Wyoming, to Denver, Colorado. I was very fortunate to be hired by Western Crude Oil, a local company. They were in the process of being consumed by Getty Oil Company and a few years later merged with Texaco.

I loved working in various aspects of the human resources department, and that's how I met Melody Reed in 1982. Melody needed to change her benefits since she was going through a divorce, and as we talked she started to sob over her situation. I finally said, "Melody, men . . . who needs 'em!" We both started laughing and have been "sisters" ever since.

I was fortunate to take an early retirement from Texaco after eighteen years, following yet another merger. After that I worked for nine years with the National Western Stock Show and Rodeo. Although a city girl, I loved this awesome experience as a cowgirl!

After working for Texaco for so long, Melody and I were always excited whenever we saw the refurbished Texaco stations along Route 66!

PHOTO COURTESY OF GLENDA "G" STONE

St. Louis

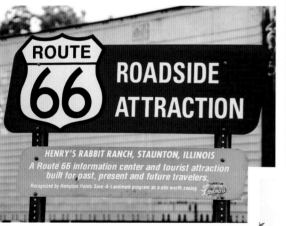

MISSOURI

fter four wonderful days meandering through the state of Illinois, the Route 66 adventure crossed into Missouri stopping first at the historic Chain of Rocks Bridge. Although it's a mere eighty-eight miles via the conventional speedway on Route 55 to our next destination in Eureka, Missouri, traveling the Mother Road and enjoying the sights along the way took all day.

Not to be missed on this leg of the trip was Henry's Rabbit Ranch & Route 66 Emporium in Staunton, Illinois. This classic Route 66 stop is a crazy collection of anything related to rabbits, including VW

Rabbit cars, several of which are buried hood first into the ground.

One of the highlights of the journey included a stop to see the giant catsup bottle water tower in Collinsville, Illinois. This 170-foot water tower was built in 1949 as part of a bottling plant that produced Brooks Catsup and was placed on the National Register of Historic Places in 2002. The building is currently for sale, including the catsup bottle!

A favorite stop for the Sisters was the Pink Elephant Antique Mall in Livingston, Illinois. Not only is it huge, it has just about anything a glamper Sister could possibly desire plus an ice cream stand! The Sisters on the Fly love to shop, so it was a little bit of heaven. Just the outside of the market was

PHOTO COURTESY OF GLENDA "G" STONE

MISSOURI

MISSOURI

enough to entice a Sister in a rush to slow down for some serious shopping. The front of the market features a giant pink elephant, a huge tricycle, and a flying saucer guaranteed to lure even the non-shopping Sister.

The final stop on the way to St. Louis was the Chain of Rocks Bridge.

Deborah Lyle Fuqua
SISTER #784

I'm lying here with tears rolling onto my pillow. My heart is full and my body is tired. I wonder how many of us "All the Way" girls released some tears this morning. The mix of emotions is overwhelming. We've traveled thousands of miles, bonding along the way. Many new friendships were made as more sisters added on. We weathered storms, floods, heat, cold, trailer repairs, injuries (thinking of you, Kathy J. Carew), emotional outbursts, tears of frustration, sleepless nights, dead-end roads, bumpy roads, and white-knuckle moments as we descended mountains and navigated six-lane interstate highways. We missed our families and pets left back home. But I wouldn't trade a minute of it. The feeling of accomplishment is something no one can take away from us. We will have stories to tell our grandchildren. And, most importantly, we did it together. We combined our strengths and talents to help each other reach this goal. Our hosts stepped up to provide us with places to rest and recover while spending fun times with our Sisters. Our brave caravan leaders got us here safely while having lots of "adventurous" moments along the way. We've learned a lot about each other and about ourselves. We did it! I love you all.

Why did I name my trailer "Happy"? Well, that was easy . . . she makes me happy! And being with my Sisters make me *happy*!

Mary Lee Block
SISTER #3186

Long before I officially joined Sisters on the Fly, I knew what I would name my vintage trailer. I had worked for a company I dearly loved . . . Eastern Air Lines. So I found a 1960 Shasta, with wings of course, and had it restored into my little first-class cabin on wheels.

The Little Eastern Flyer took me on an unbelievable trip this spring with my amazing Sisters. We traveled the entire Route 66, the Main Street of America. She showed me sights I had never seen, taught me how to do things I never thought I could, and introduced me to folks I shall never forget.

MISSOURI

From 1929 to 1967, this bridge was the primary crossing of the Mississippi River on Route 66. In 1998, the bridge was renovated for pedestrian and bicycle use and is now a favorite stop among Route 66 travelers. At 5,353 feet long, it is the longest pedestrian/bicycle bridge in the country.

As the caravans of Sisters found their way to the bridge, the parking lot filled with our trailers. With a misty rain falling, we made our way across the bridge, taking pictures, some walking and others riding bikes.

Then we were on our way to Eureka, Missouri, where fifty-seven Sisters gathered at the St. Louis West/Historic Route 66 KOA campground for two nights. Deb Morse, Sister #5427, did a great job coordinating this stop in the Show Me State.

PHOTO COURTESY OF SUSAN FORD-WEST

The second evening we were treated to a homemade supper by Ellen Franks, Sister #548.

Next to the campground was the Missouri Route 66

"This was an inspiring event that I wanted to be part of. I wanted to challenge myself to go a long distance in my trailer—to be independent. I looked forward to meeting new Sisters and having fun with old Sisters. I was so happy to see the country! I was very sad that I couldn't go all the way. This was the best time I have ever had with the Sisters."
—SANDRA OSKO, SISTER #3077

PHOTO COURTESY OF SUSAN FORD-WEST

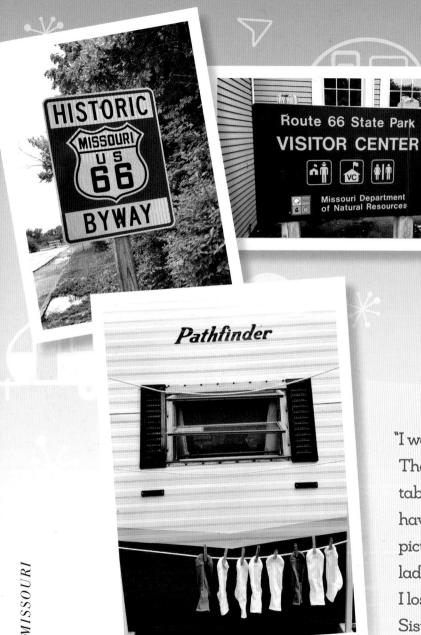

"I was overwhelmed with the women who are members. They are from all walks of life and bring so much to the table. I was very sad leaving my new friends. I wish I could have done the whole trip, but have enjoyed seeing the pictures. I think I can be a better Sister to our Minnesota ladies and hope to see our membership grow. Last year I lost my sister to cancer. Now I have over 6,000 new Sisters."—SUE NOTCH, SISTER #5143

State Park Visitor Center. Several of the Sisters enjoyed browsing the gift shop and learning about the vital role Missouri has played in the restoration and preservation of the Mother Road.

PHOTO COURTESY OF LEEANN BENNETT

After five rainy days, we were overjoyed to have a full day of sunshine to explore St. Louis. Just about everyone saw the Gateway Arch—it's hard to miss because it dominates the St. Louis skyline. Several Sisters went to the St. Louis Zoo, some to the botanical garden, and others to historic St. Charles for some great shopping along the brick-paved streets.

PHOTO COURTESY OF SUSAN FORD-WEST

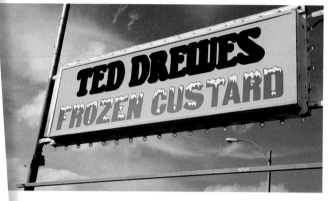

Since 1941, Ted Drewes Frozen Custard has been a classic Route 66 roadside attraction. It invented the famous "concrete" (a thick malt or shake served upside down) and is as popular today as it was in 1921.

After careful planning for the next segment of the journey, the Sisters were off to Stop #4—Springfield, Missouri.

Springfield

We lined up our trailers in true "Sister style" to caravan from the St. Louis West/Historic Route 66 KOA in Eureka, Missouri, to the next destination, Springfield, Missouri, home of the original Bass Pro Shops, the granddaddy of all outdoor stores. We passed many motels on Main Street USA, but the Skylark caught our eye. Located in St. Clair, Missouri, it has an original neon sign and is a participant in the Route 66 Corridor Preservation Program.

One of the first stops for many of the Sisters was Meramec Caverns. Referred to as "America's Cave," it houses the rarest and largest cave formations in the world. The caverns are the largest commercial caves in the state of Missouri— well worth the scenic exit in Stanton, Missouri.

For those Sisters who worked up an appetite on their journey through the caverns, there was a treat waiting in the quaint village of Bourbon. First, though, we completed a search for the three unique water towers of Bourbon. Yes, they really do supply the town with water and not bourbon!

Next we eagerly headed to the Circle N (Inn), a throwback to the original burger and malt shops that surely dotted the landscape of days gone by on the Mother Road from east to west. As we took our seats at the diner-style tables, a local resident came by to welcome us to town and tell us the story of her four generations of family in Bourbon. One more experience of Route 66 hospitality and pride!

Paulette Roth

SISTER #249

"Joy" is the word that I would use to describe our trip—pure joy. If I wasn't feeling very joyful at any given moment, all I had to do was look around at a Sister on a stick pony wearing a petticoat or hula hooping or singing karaoke and I could not help but smile. Then there were the moments of joy that came from accomplishment and overcoming a challenge: a trailer pushed out of the mud, a Sister returning to the caravan after a breakdown, a group of thirty Sisters standing on the Santa Monica Pier. There is the joy of sisterly friendship—the smile you get from another Sister who hasn't seen you for a while or a Sister who makes you laugh during a challenging situation or the one who puts a hand, or quilt, on your shoulder and says, "Everything's going to be OK."

Ten years ago I saw the Sisters camped out at "The Farm" in South Phoenix. When I saw the trailers, I knew in an instant I was going to join this group. I visited Maurrie at her home to sign up and ask how to find a trailer. One week later I had a 1961 Shasta with the original interior. It was so 1960s I had to give it a name from that time period. I altered a song name from 1961, SugarPieHoneyBun, and gave her a diner theme.

I told—not asked—my husband that I was doing the entire Route 66 trip from our Phoenix home. It was not on my bucket list, but met my need for adventure, challenge, and self-reliance. The best part of the trip was all the like-minded gals. We are a can-get-it-done group that just wants to have fun. A whole lot of fun is what we had. Yahoo! Life is good.

MISSOURI

MISSOURI

Once the gridlock of all our trailers parked every which way outside the diner was undone, we were able to venture toward the "City of Murals," Cuba, Missouri. Some couldn't resist the great barbecue offered by the Missouri Hick Bar-B-Q, and Connie, the owner of the adjacent Wagon Wheel Motel, which continues to accommodate eager tourists on the Mother Road, was happy to have us visit.

As we approached Fanning, Missouri, some of the Sisters looked forward to that special photo op in the World's Largest Rocking Chair known as "The Route 66 Rocker." It was a great place to rest while surveying what the Fanning 66 Outpost had to offer tourists.

Arriving in Springfield came with the promise of a pizza dinner and two days of activities organized by the SOTF hostesses, Denise Davis, Sister #4163, Helen Elston, Sister #99 and their assistants. We gathered that evening and shared stories of all the

places we had stopped and the unique experiences we had had with our caravans that day along the historic route. Plans were finalized for the following day's activities.

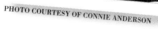

The plans included a quick trip to Branson, Missouri, for those Sisters interested in glamour, glitz, and shopping. After all, Branson is home to Dick's Oldtime 5 & 10, described as the "Last of an American Tradition."

Those who didn't take the side trip to Branson had plenty of shopping opportunities at the original Bass Pro Shop in Springfield, with four floors of goodies to entice members of the largest outdoor organization for women—Sisters on the Fly. The Sisters have held meetups and rallies, luncheons and shopping sprees, and workshops and demos at Bass Pro Shops and

MISSOURI

Linda Scott

SISTER #1578

PHOTO COURTESY OF DEBRA FUQUA

I am Sister #1578 towing the 2010 pop-up Chalet. I recently celebrated my seventieth birthday. I never liked the term "bucket list." I prefer to think about how to live every day of the life I'm given—a life list. Seeing more of my own home country is on my life list. And, oh, how surprised I was to discover what a beautiful country it is.

Now that I'm home and well and the chores are nearly finished and the trailer nearly clean, I'm remembering the fun and great times and not much of the strife. I remember walking like an Egyptian and rocking out multiple times to "Mustang Sally." I remember the Meramec Caverns in Missouri and meeting the mayor of Williams, Arizona. I remember Elvis in the women's bathrooms along the way. I remember feeling hope and expectation in Chicago and exuberance on the Santa Monica Pier.

I want to see more of Illinois and Missouri, and I think Oklahoma deserves another chance without the torrential rains. I fooled around and missed Winslow, Arizona. So would I do it all again? Give me two years to think about it.

When I arrived in Joliet, I was alone. Ellen Franks found that I did not have a caravan to join and immediately invited me to join the group of women she was with. The other women, Kayo Downey, Pam Poindexter, and Jehnet Carlson, included me as though I had been in their group from the beginning!

PHOTO COURTESY OF CINDI MLADENKA

Cabella's all over the country, so we were right at home at the granddaddy of them all. After a visit to the Springfield Route 66 Visitor Center, the Sisters were ready to greet the citizens of Galena, Kansas, who were eagerly awaiting the opportunity to share their 13.2 miles of the Main Street of America with us.

PHOTO COURTESY OF CONNIE ANDERSON

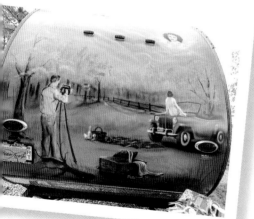

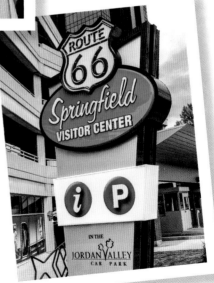

PHOTO COURTESY OF SUSAN FORD-WEST

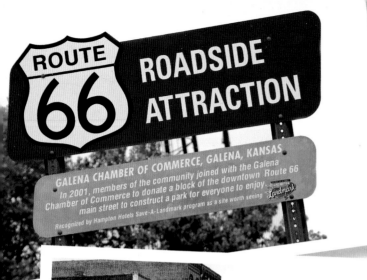

ROUTE 66 ROADSIDE ATTRACTION

GALENA CHAMBER OF COMMERCE, GALENA, KANSAS
In 2001, members of the community joined with the Galena Chamber of Commerce to donate a block of the downtown Route 66 main street to construct a park for everyone to enjoy. *Landmark*
Recognized by Hampton Hotels Save-A-Landmark program as a site worth seeing

Kansas

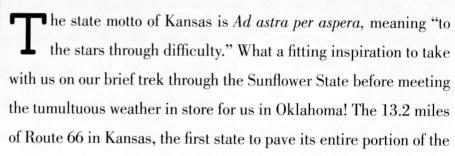

The state motto of Kansas is *Ad astra per aspera,* meaning "to the stars through difficulty." What a fitting inspiration to take with us on our brief trek through the Sunflower State before meeting the tumultuous weather in store for us in Oklahoma! The 13.2 miles of Route 66 in Kansas, the first state to pave its entire portion of the historic route in 1929, rolled out the red carpet for the Sisters on the Fly on May 20, 2015.

The first stop on the Kansas Mother Road was Galena. Main Street was closed that morning in anticipation of the arrival of the sixty-six Sisters expected from Joplin, Missouri, where we had gathered to begin the caravan into Galena. The city welcomed us with open arms and warm hearts. The mayor of Galena

closed the highway for this historic event, and volunteers assisted the Sisters with parking trailers on the main streets of this

quaint little town, which served as the inspiration for the community of "Radiator Springs" in the Pixar movie *Cars*. The local press interviewed several of the Sisters, and our story was broadcast on the local news from Joplin, Missouri, that evening. Many of the Sisters stopped to take pictures at the iconic "Cars on the Route," the home of Tow Mater, one of the characters in *Cars*, inspired by the 1951 International boom truck parked alongside the restored gas station.

We were invited to gather at the gazebo at Howard "Pappy" Litchfield Park, part of the historic Will Rogers Highway, as Route 66 is known in Kansas, to share in a lunch prepared by local SOTF hostesses Lori Thompson, Sister #1990, Terry Dykstra, Sister #113, Pam Wilcott, Sister #113, and their volunteers. The townspeople

Glenda "G" Stone

SISTER #62

Like so many Sisters, when I found Sisters on the Fly, I thought the little trailers were so cute. I had to have one. I love being outdoors: the smell of the campfire, listening to the sounds of the creek, wind, and animals. I love camping! I love my trailers! I've had four. I still have my first one—the Circle G! Bunkhouse. I've sold two of them, and my last one is called Bezos. I named her after the original owners, Norman and Lois Beze. They bought her in 1954 and camped in her until 1999. She was kept in their garage until she was noticed by my friend Chris, who bought her, cleaned her up, and sold her to me. We drove from Arkansas to California to pick her up. So it was perfect for her to take a trip on Route 66 and end up in California again.

Until joining SOTF, I had never been confident enough to take off alone. I'd not been away from family for any period of time, and had certainly never pulled a trailer! My first "outing" was to take off with new Sister-friend, Debra, Sister #23, leaving from Little Rock, Arkansas, and headed to "Cowgirl College" in Phoenix, Arizona! We were gone sixteen days. It was scary, exciting, big fun, and still some of the best memories. I learned self-confidence, and that I could actually take care of myself. I overcame my fear of basically everything on that trip. I met Maurrie and Becky, Sisters #1 and #2, learned to hitch a trailer and saddle a trail horse; had "Rocco," the original head of Arizona Cowboy College, say my throwing of a lasso was a "thing of beauty"; saw rattlesnakes in the desert; and pulled my first little trailer up the mountain out of Oak Creek Canyon in Sedona, Arizona, without dying!

When talk first started about the Route 66 trip, I told my husband about it and he said, "You gotta do it—the whole thing." So many things had to fall into place for me to be able to go. The chance to be with so many of the Sisters that I had only met through the SOTF social media and to travel with more Sisters than had ever assembled for an event before, finishing up with possibly 300-plus Sisters in California—I just couldn't *not* go.

It was a trip of a lifetime, and not just for me, but for so many I met along the way. I'm Sister #62 and have been on many adventures with SOTF since joining twelve years ago. This was the biggest event we've ever had. I *had* to do it! I was out of my comfort level and challenged several times on the trip. Being away from family and friends for thirty days was crazy. But we all survived! It was a great adventure!

Traveling down some of the oldest, "original" sections of Route 66, sometimes running out of pavement and wondering if we were somewhere we really shouldn't be, and then popping out at a historical marker to learn that the road we had just been on was decommissioned in 1937 are great memories . . . now that we know we survived it! It was epic!

PHOTO COURTESY OF GLENDA "G" STONE

personally welcomed us to their lovely little town of 3,000 citizens, looked at our trailers parked throughout their downtown, and wished us well on the rest of our journey westward. Galena will always remember the Sisters who came to town—and we'll never forget Galena.

Our next stop was Riverton, Kansas, famous for Eisler Brothers Old Riverton Store, which claims to be the oldest continuously operating business on Route 66. If you're lucky, like the Sisters were on this particular day, you'll meet Dean, who will show you his amazing double-jointed ankle trick! All the Sisters very much enjoyed visiting this landmark 1925 soda fountain, a throwback to the general store days.

The final stop in Kansas was Baxter Springs. When the caravan arrived in town, Sue Gast, co-owner of Angels on the Route, treated all of us to a free cup of frozen custard. Children stood on the corner with

welcome signs, and local business owners and citizens came out to chat about our trip and our trailers. In just a few hours, we fell in love with the smallest piece of the Mother Road with the biggest heart! We drove across the border into Oklahoma eating our sunflower cookies and knowing that the Sunflower State had been a bright spot on the Mother Road.

Linda Boyett Greeve
SISTER # 4547

I knew when I retired that I wanted to travel and see as much of our beautiful country as I could. I loved the idea of camping. I googled "women traveling alone," and Sisters on the Fly was one of the sites that came up. I loved the "rules" and made contact with the local wrangler. She set up a meet and greet with a few other Sisters, and by the end of lunch I was hooked! I went right home and signed up!

When I decided to buy a camper, I chose to get a new one so I would have a warranty and room for grandkids who want to camp once in a while. Traveling Route 66 was among the plans I had—and what better way to do it than with the SOTF instead of on my own. There are so many amazing women in this group, and I now have some lifelong Sisters!

I named my camper Madame Butterfly in honor of my mom, who passed away in February 2008. That was her CB handle years ago, and she always loved butterflies. On every trip I take, I always see at least one butterfly, so I know she is traveling with me.

Pam Forde Asher
SISTER #2551

One of my dreams: To travel across our beautiful country . . . stopping along the way to see historic places. To travel the road that was built to get to the West years ago!

To be independent, able to say, "I can do this!" To get to know people in many different states across the country.

This was an awesome experience, and Sisters on the Fly gave me this opportunity.

KANSAS

"After I joined SOTF I bought my trailer from another Sister in Kansas. My 1959 Oasis is named Toto's Tin Can, representing the great state of Kansas with sunflowers painted all over her. In the last four years, I have discovered all that I can do myself, stretched myself to face a few fears, and had more excitement in my life than I could ever imagine! Who wouldn't want to claim 6,000+ Sisters who love and support you beyond your wildest dreams?"—LORI THOMPSON, SISTER #1990

Claremore

Eighty-three Sisters on the Fly pulled into Will Rogers Downs KOA in Claremore, Oklahoma, after spending an eventful afternoon on Main Street USA. The first historic stop was Commerce, the home of Mickey Mantle and a few iconic Route 66 attractions.

Allen's Fillin' Station provided a great backdrop for the Sisters' vintage trailers, and a few stopped for ice cream before taking a ride on the wild side—the Route 66 Ribbon Road!

Leaving Commerce there is a small sign indicating a right turn to follow "Old Route 66." The caravan, led by Karen West, Sister #3119, followed the turn to the right. The paved road soon became gravel and

OKLAHOMA

"I can't pull my 1965 Shasta any more because my tow vehicle was rusted out due to the winters in Illinois. So I decided to give myself permission to take a little loan from my 401K and build my own trailer from the ground up. I bought a trailer kit from Harbor Freight and plans on how to build one on the Internet. I changed the design and made it my own. I can even sleep out under the stars; I just pull the strings to draw the vinyl back. It even has a fireplace—just fake, but it's wonderful. It's decked out with cowgirl stuff. Just because I'm a woman doesn't mean I can't build a trailer."—EMETA KRAEMER, SISTER #677

*SEE PAGE 12 FOR PICTURE OF EMETA'S TRAILER.

OKLAHOMA

gradually transitioned to dirt. With nowhere to turn around, the caravan continued, and after a few miles a small ribbon of pavement reappeared in the middle of this one-lane dusty road. Finally reaching a cross road, we discovered a marble road marker on the left describing the historic road we had just traveled.

Once we arrived safely in Claremore, the local hostesses, Carolyn Cundiff, Sister #2455, Lori Kuntz, Sister #553, and Skeeter Chilton, Sister #605, arranged our

welcome dinner at the Will Rogers Memorial Museum.

The museum also provided a theatre program that included a performance by their resident Will Rogers impersonator, Andy Hogan, who presented a lively interpretation of the wit and wisdom of one of Oklahoma's favorite sons.

Karen West

SISTER #3119

PHOTO COURTESY OF SUSAN FORD-WEST

I joined SOTF in the fall of 2012. My trailer is a 1960 Shasta called the Little Red Diner. I've had her since 2009 and lived in her nearly full time for five years. I've learned that it's possible to thrive in sixty square feet. Living small is very liberating. Two years ago, Susan joined me, and a year ago, Butch, our fifteen-pound toy poodle puppy moved in. The Diner is getting smaller every day, and we're ready to move back into our house in Kansas City, Missouri, this fall.

I'm a professional photographer specializing in intimate landscapes and national parks. Trees, rocks, and sand are my preferred subjects. The preservation of Route 66 is a project of the National Park Service. When I saw the Route 66 SOTF announcement, I knew immediately that I wanted to do the entire trip, photograph it, and do this book to document the adventure. I didn't realize at the time how great a professional challenge it would be.

One of the reasons I like to photograph trees, rocks, and sand is because they

PHOTO COURTESY OF SUSAN FORD-WEST

don't complain—it's also the reason I prefer not to photograph people. I have a great deal of concern about publishing this book—I could become the most disliked Sister when my pictures of the Sisters on the Fly are revealed. I offer my most humble apology here.

My best day on the trip was May 20. We spent the afternoon in Galena, Kansas, and I photographed the caravan driving into town. I couldn't stop smiling and giggling to myself as the trailers kept rolling down Main Street. I think I took over 300 pictures that day. As we moved into Oklahoma, a small caravan of Sisters asked me to take the lead. They didn't know about my very poor sense of direction, but I boldly agreed. I followed a sign pointing to "Old Route 66" and soon after the turn, we were on a gravel road that quickly turned into a dirt road. With six trailers behind me, there was no place to turn around. After about five miles, the dirt road turned into what had once been a narrow paved road. It was a bit bumpy with old potholes and missing pavement and a couple of cows and a donkey in a field observing our progress.

Finally, we reached the end of the road, to find a marble plaque on the left. I jumped out of the van to discover that we had been on Route 66's historic Ribbon Road, aka Sidewalk Highway. It was completed in 1922 and taken out of commission in 1937! I nearly fell over laughing. As the Sisters behind me got out of their vehicles, we laughed and laughed and gathered around for a group picture. Soon, another caravan pulled in behind us. It's a day I will never forget.

Susan Spinti, Sister #5376, traveled the Mother Road in her Prius. An "All the Way" Sister, she transformed the Prius into a camping machine worthy of respect by all. We think she should submit her designs to Toyota to develop the all-new Camprius.

ATW Sister Jehnet Carlson, Sister #4269, left the road in Santa Fe because of a family emergency. Jehnet always had the right tool in an emergency, including a tow truck. Her kind and generous spirit was missed.

All the Way Sister #1975, Sarah Mcmurray is a retired farrier and a full time RVer in her 2011 26-foot Echo New Generation trailer. A long time SOTF, she enjoyed meeting up with old friends and meeting new Sisters along the road.

OKLAHOMA

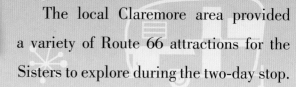

The local Claremore area provided a variety of Route 66 attractions for the Sisters to explore during the two-day stop. Some went to Foyil to take a look at the World's Largest Totem Pole, which was created with rebar and cement.

Others ventured out to the famous Blue Whale in Catoosa. The day was cloudy, but those carrying cameras were able to get pictures of the whale and its reflection on the water at this iconic roadside attraction built in the 1970s and now considered a "must-see" on the route.

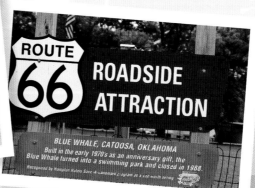

Those who lingered in the campground were surprised to find the Budweiser Clydesdales gracefully cantering through with their trainers and Dalmation. It didn't take long for the word to spread and the Sisters to emerge from their trailers with cameras in hand, ready to pet these gentle giants.

"I didn't have a life plan to ever do this. It was never on my bucket list. I just signed up for a few stops, but I wish now I would have gone the entire way. Nothing compares to traveling with Sisters on the Fly. The camaraderie, the support, the down-home fun and adventure were abundant. We came from different backgrounds, ethnic groups, races, sexual preferences, and social status, but none of that mattered. We bonded as a family. We pushed each other toward higher potential and overlooked each other's weaknesses. We looked out for each other, assisting with physical strength, mechanical needs, and even emotional support. We built a trust that nobody would be left behind. It honestly was a life-changing experience for me."—CONNIE ANDERSON, SISTER #1275

OKLAHOMA

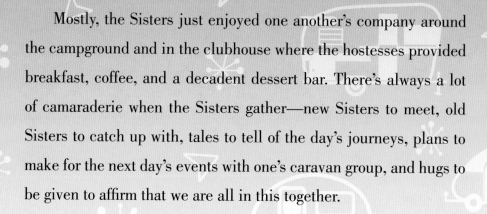

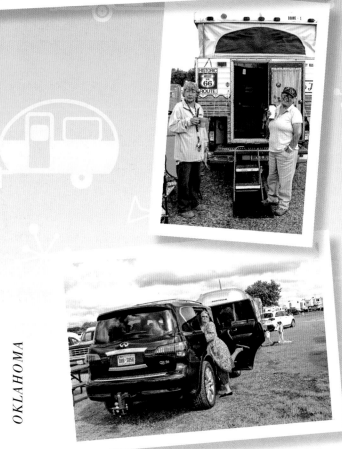

Mostly, the Sisters just enjoyed one another's company around the campground and in the clubhouse where the hostesses provided breakfast, coffee, and a decadent dessert bar. There's always a lot of camaraderie when the Sisters gather—new Sisters to meet, old Sisters to catch up with, tales to tell of the day's journeys, plans to make for the next day's events with one's caravan group, and hugs to be given to affirm that we are all in this together.

"I love SOTF and everything it stands for. I have met wonderful people. I have camped for over forty years. My kids are grown and my spouse is not ready to retire yet, so this has been my 'me' time. My camper's name is Fernweh. It's German for 'far sickness,' the desire to travel."
—CATHY COODY, SISTER #5089

OKLAHOMA

chapter 7

Oklahoma City

PHOTO COURTESY OF SUSAN FORD-WEST

After a great gathering in Claremore, the Sisters hit the road for Oklahoma City—straight into the heart of Tornado Alley. From the beginning of the trip, we had experienced rain and cool weather, but nothing could have prepared us for the severe weather we met in Oklahoma City! It didn't stop us from living the SOTF motto, however: "We have more fun than anyone!"

The journey from Claremore to Oklahoma City on America's Main Street had many Route 66 highlights. The first stop was Tulsa, which spans twenty-four miles of old Route 66.

The Meadow Gold Milk and Ice Cream sign is an epic landmark. It was restored and returned to the Tulsa skyline in 2009.

One of the highlights of the day was the Rock Cafe in Stroud, Oklahoma. The building was constructed in 1939 out of local stone.

OKLAHOMA

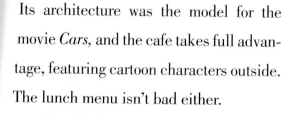

Its architecture was the model for the movie *Cars,* and the cafe takes full advantage, featuring cartoon characters outside. The lunch menu isn't bad either.

The Skyliner Motel in Stroud is a classic Route 66 icon still in service with the original neon sign.

Next stop was Davenport, Oklahoma, home to several iconic Route 66 memories. Several Sisters stopped at Rustic Sisters and posed for pictures at the cowgirl-themed marquee.

Chandler, Oklahoma, features the Route 66 Interpretive Museum, the Phillips 66 Station, and the Lincoln Motel. The Sisters cruised through town, taking pictures and stopping to visit the sights.

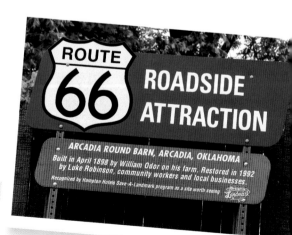

Nearly all the Sisters stopped to visit the Round Barn in Arcadia, Oklahoma. Built in 1898, it is still considered an architectural wonder and is reported to be the most photographed sight on Route 66.

The last stop before arriving at the state capital—and one the Sisters were most looking forward to—was POPS. This soda pop shop and restaurant opened in 2007 and has become a favorite landmark on Route 66. The road sign is a giant soda pop bottle that is sixty-six feet tall and weighs four tons.

The interior glass walls are lined with shelves of multicolored pop bottles of every variety imaginable.

The Sisters singlehandedly attempted to purchase nearly every flavor possible.

OKLAHOMA

Kathleen Doty & Eileen Billey

SISTER #4816   SISTER #4541

Eileen heard about SOTF in June 2013. She had a 1978 Shasta trailer that had belonged to her mother and was sitting in her brother's hay field. Eileen and I have been best friends for sixty-five years and are true sisters of the heart.

She invited me to go on a Meetup in March 2014 in Connellsville, Pennsylvania, with the Mid-Atlantic Sisters. Since her Shasta was unavailable, we took her family's Winnebago—Marshmallow—all thirty-three feet of her. We set up camp at Rivers Edge Campground and were awakened very early the next morning to find the river's edge at our front door. So started the show— the "Sister saga"—of Eileen and Kathleen.

Eileen mentioned the Route 66 trip, and once we started talking about it we decided that we were going "all the way." We both own vintage trailers that are currently being restored, so Marshmallow got the nod to go on Route 66. This adventure was a real learning experience for us. Eileen surprised herself with how well she was able to handle Marshmallow. We visited many places we had never been before and met so many wonderful Sisters who gave us a helping hand along the way. We hope to have many more adventures with this wonderful group. Thank you, Karen and Susan, for all the work you are doing to record this wonderful memory.

"I first saw Sisters on the Fly at the Country Living Show in Ohio in 2010 and thought, 'Wow, this is for me!' I grew up camping and traveling all over the United States. My husband and I did the same with our children. But it took four years for me to join, and I'm kicking myself now! I purchased a 1969 Lakeland and had it repaired, ready to travel Route 66. This was my first outing in Lil Gracie. It's named after my grandmother Grace, who was always the first one in the ocean or lake, telling us how 'invigorating' the water was! She would have loved this!"

—BONNIE SHAFTO, SISTER #5380

Finally, after traveling a grueling 136 miles, 105 Sisters on the Fly gathered at the Oklahoma State Fairgrounds for two nights of camping and doing what we do best, "having more fun than anyone!" At check-in, it was merely raining. The weather was inconsequential, however, because the SOTF hostesses DeAnn Merritt Parham, Sister #3853, Becky Rickard, Sister #3886 and Jackie Lachance-Henry, Sister #2274 put together an amazing variety of events to keep the Sisters indoors and busy.

That evening we were invited to a special dinner hosted by the vendors at The Rink, an old skating rink with 28,000 square feet of antiques, furniture, and an assortment of memorabilia from over 100 dealers and artisans. It was a perfect opportunity for the Sisters to shop and enjoy a hot dog dinner with all the fixins.

The next morning we were treated to breakfast and a docent tour of the National Cowboy & Western Heritage Museum, the premier home of Western art and

OKLAHOMA

PHOTO COURTESY OF SUSAN FORD-WEST

artifacts. It features a collection of works by Frederic Remington, Charles M. Russell, and sculptor James Earle Fraser's *The End of the Trail.*

PHOTO COURTESY OF SUSAN FORD-WEST

After breakfast the Sisters visited a variety of Oklahoma City's shopping highlights and the Oklahoma City National Memorial & Museum, a place of "quiet reflection."

A highlight of the day was an invitation to participate in the Oklahoma Gay Rodeo Association (OGRA) Grand Entry Promenade at the fairgrounds. We were encouraged to wear our "sister finery and wave!" The stick pony races were canceled the previous evening due to weather, so the participants brought their ponies to the rodeo. The OGRA had never seen such a sight or had so much fun. The Sisters loved every minute of it!

OKLAHOMA

That evening, dinner was held at the Cattlemen's Café. Welcome to Oklahoma—Tornado Alley! Those at the cafe could see the rain coming down in sheets, but were able to wait until it passed before leaving for the fairgrounds.

A few Sisters, however, had decided to forgo dinner and were at the campground when the tornado sirens started blasting and the fairground staff came through telling them to evacuate to the shelter. Leaving trailers and valuables behind, the brave and fun-loving Sisters hurried to the basement of the big hall to wait for the all-clear signal.

When the diners returned, the campground was filled with big pools of water and mud, and most Sisters hitched up and headed for local hotels and higher ground. A few brave souls stayed behind, hoping for clear skies and the ability to pull out of the mud in the morning.

At first light, the water had receded, but the grounds were still a muddy mess. In true Sister style, all remaining trailers were hitched up, pulled out of the mud, and on their way to Texas with good humor—and hopes of finding a trailer wash down the road.

Amarillo

One hundred twenty-eight Sisters gathered at the Amarillo Ranch RV Park. The 257-mile transition from stormy Oklahoma to the heat of Texas was a welcome change, and there had been plenty of classic Route 66 attractions along the way.

The first stop was El Reno, Oklahoma. For most modern travelers, El Reno is a forgotten stop a few miles off Interstate 40. During the days of Route 66, however, it was a great place to rest, eat, and gas up. The town still celebrates its Mother Road heritage.

Lucille's Service Station in Hydro, Oklahoma, was built in 1929. It was named for Lucille Hamons, who ran the business for sixty years. She had a reputation for being friendly to all who

stopped at her station, gaining the nickname "Mother of the Mother Road." She would have made a great Sister on the Fly.

The Oklahoma Route 66 Museum opened in 1995 in Clinton, Oklahoma. Several of the Sisters stopped at the museum to explore the historical significance of Oklahoma's Will Rogers Highway.

Not far down the road is Elk City, home to the National Route 66 Museum. This museum has exhibits and artifacts from the eight states that Route 66 traverses. It also includes a variety of other exhibits such as vintage cars and Oklahoma farm and ranch equipment.

Lisa Mora, Sister #2348, arranged for a special meeting with Harley at his Curiosity Shop in Erick, Oklahoma. She guaranteed that we would not be disappointed with the amazing assortment of goodies in his shop or his

Sharon Lambert
SISTER #508

I joined SOTF ten years ago after reading about them in *Country Living Magazine*. I told my sister, Nan, also a Sister, that if the group ever got to Texas, I wanted to join. She showed me this fantastic story accompanied by great color photos in the paper about the interstate closing for the Sisters caravanning through Fort Worth.

I had sold antiques for years, so I wanted to buy a trailer that would hold its value. I bought a beautiful, original, vintage Airstream, and when I took it to my first event, the Round Top Antiques Fair, I realized I owned a beautiful trailer that I couldn't "Sister up." I stored it for a year and then sold it to another Sister. I knew I was not comfortable towing seventeen feet, so my next trailer was Sweet Fanny Magee, a 1964 Meztendorf that would fit into a garage. I kept her for a couple years and then made a road trip to New Jersey with three Sisters to pick up a 1964 Shasta Compact, which became Kaula the Wild. I was getting into this theme-decorating thing and wanted to try my hand at a Gypsy Wagon, but as everyone knows, Gypsy Wagons need rear doors, a rare thing in a vintage trailer. I finally found one for sale and hightailed it to Oregon from Tennessee to pick it up. I sold the Shasta Compact to a banjo playing man in Texas who traveled to music events. He sold it to a Texas Sister who traveled in it full time for a couple of years.

A Sister friend, Fran Rattay, Sister #487, returned to Tennessee with me and made some fantastic curtains for my other trailer, Packin' Polly, and a local high school art teacher painted the Gypsy Wagon (he had also painted Kaula the Wild). So I had two trailers now: a twelve-foot Gypsy and a sixteen-foot Cardinal named Packin' Polly. I sold the Gypsy, but I loved the space in Polly. Planning for the Route 66 trip was under way, and I knew I wanted a bathroom for that long a trip. I had no doubt that I was going "all the way." I sold Polly in the summer of 2014 and bought my 2008 T@DA, Goldie, my first new trailer. I love Goldie!

She made the trip just fine, with a few minor glitches. I don't plan to ever part with her! Next January, Goldie and I plan to spend the month in Quartzsite, Arizona. I am currently learning about solar panels. Traveling with a trailer is a real learning experience. I have ten years of mistakes and errors that I wouldn't trade for anything. It took me ten years to graduate to being comfortable towing something as long as Goldie. She is eighteen and a half feet long. That's a big difference from those twelve-foot trailers!

Packin' Polly and the Gypsy Wagon were both pictured in the book *Glamping with Mary Jane,* and the Gypsy had a fantastic write-up by Lisa Mora in her *Vintage Caravan Magazine.*

rendition of "Get Your Kicks on Route 66." As the crowd gathered, Harley, dressed in his classic red-and-white-striped overalls, greeted us with overwhelming enthusiasm and pointed out the special features of his shop. Once the Sisters were seated, Harley took his place front and center, picked up his guitar, shared his heartfelt story of losing his wife, Annabelle, who had passed two years earlier, then broke into the most joyful rendition of "Get Your Kicks" we had ever heard.

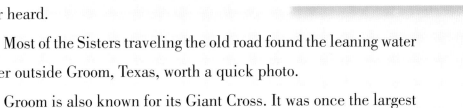

Most of the Sisters traveling the old road found the leaning water tower outside Groom, Texas, worth a quick photo.

Groom is also known for its Giant Cross. It was once the largest cross in the Western Hemisphere, but that record was broken in 2001 when a bigger cross was erected in Effingham, Illinois.

A favorite stop along the road was conceived by a group of hippies called the Ant Farm from San Francisco. It's a public art display known as the Cadillac Ranch, where ten Cadillacs are buried hood first into the Texas dirt. Over the years, they have been torn apart and spray-painted by Route 66 enthusiasts so many times that it's guaranteed anything painted one day will most likely be covered over the next. The day the Sisters visited the site, the cars were surrounded by pools of thick mud from recent rains, but it didn't deter a few from wading in with their cans of Krylon to document the visit by the Sisters on the Fly.

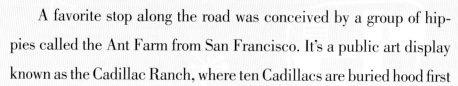

"Twenty years ago I saw the cutest campers on the cover of *Country Living Magazine*. It made me smile. Oh, how I wished to be part of the SOTF. At the time, I was single, raising three kids, and working two jobs. I didn't think I'd ever be part of this group, but I never forgot the fun of seeing that caravan of campers in the magazine. I only attended two Route 66 stops, but what a *grand* experience. We truly had more fun than anyone. Thanks for the memories, Sisters!"
—VICKIE PANNELL, SISTER #4044, "POPPY'S GIRL"

We arrived at the Amarillo Ranch RV Park hungry. Our hostesses, Cindy Salmon, Sister #3272, and Cheryl Bass, Sister #3180, had a full lineup of fun and food to keep us entertained and fed during our two-night stay in the center of the Texas Panhandle.

Everything is BIG in Texas, and a stop in Amarillo wouldn't be complete without dinner at the Big Texan. The beer garden at the Big Texan Steak Ranch was reserved for the Sisters, and limousines transported us in luxury from the RV park on the first evening for dinner, dancing, and visiting with friends old and new.

TEXAS

TEXAS

On Saturday, the Sisters scattered around Amarillo to see the sights. Most went to the Historic Route 66 neighborhood, which features historic buildings with antiques, craft, and specialty shops and restaurants.

The last night in Amarillo, we were treated to a burger cookout at the RV park catered by the Big Texan. Of course, it featured the biggest burgers ever seen! A local country band entertained us while we dined, visited, and planned for the next day's journey to Santa Fe.

Cindi Mladenka

SISTER #3803

I've always been a fan of Route 66 and all it represents. When my husband and I celebrated our thirty-third anniversary, I posted on Facebook: "33 x 2 = 66—For our thirty-third anniversary, the two of us are going to do a little Route 66 Remembrance." We didn't get very far, but the little we saw, in the Texas Panhandle, made me want more!

When this trip was being discussed by the SOTF last summer, I knew I had to go. I asked my husband if he would ever want to do the entire trip with me sometime, and he said, "No." That's when I knew I would have to find a way to go—no matter what.

I'm proud and happy to say that I was the only native Texan to do the entire trip as an "All the Way" Sister, from Joliet, Illinois, to Santa Monica, California! From my home in West Texas, up to Chicago, down Route 66, and back to West Texas, I clocked in at thirty-three days and 5,325.3 miles! What a magnificent, memorable ride!

I don't remember when I first heard of Sisters on the Fly. I must have seen them on television, but the moment I learned of this group of adventurous women, I knew I had to be part of it. That was over twelve years ago.

When my last child graduated and left for college, I wanted to join that very day. I didn't know a soul in the organization, and I knew I wanted and needed to have my own trailer to fully participate. It took me three years to find my 1969 Spot vintage trailer in Houston, which I named The West Texas Wanderer, and I joined in June 2012.

Knowing this was my next chapter in life, I wanted my trailer to represent me—that little redheaded girl that I used to be. It was nostalgic for me—going back to my roots. This trailer meant the world to me, and it was my opportunity to be me.

After miles and miles of travel, The Wanderer eventually had to be put out to pasture. I was fortunate that her new little sister, a 2015 reissued Shasta called Texas Tiki Hut, was able to go on the cross-country adventure with me. Being her virgin voyage, she was christened with champagne upon arrival in Ventura.

When asked if I would do it all over again, I can only say, "maybe." This one-time-chance-of-a-lifetime trip can't be replicated. My memories have been made, however, there are still so many places on Route 66 that I would like to go back and visit for much more than a day. Until that time, I encourage everyone to take the opportunity to get on the road. Go out and explore this great country! There's no better way to spend a day, a week, or, in my case, a month. Happy trails!

TEXAS

Santa Fe

H eading west from Amarillo came with the excitement of
arriving at Midpoint—halfway between Chicago and Santa
Monica. Some Sisters had downloaded a smartphone app called
Road Trip 66, which describes all the attractions along the route,

pinpointing them on the roadway and in relation to the interstate highways that had long since replaced the Mother Road. There were many planned stops and some options for the final stretch into Santa Fe, each caravan deciding on its unique destination points for the day's journey. One hundred sixty-five Sisters would circle up the wagons at the Santa Fe Skies RV Park.

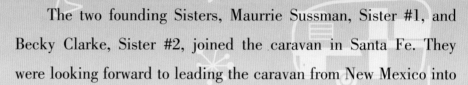

The two founding Sisters, Maurrie Sussman, Sister #1, and Becky Clarke, Sister #2, joined the caravan in Santa Fe. They were looking forward to leading the caravan from New Mexico into Maurrie's home state of Arizona. Sister #3, Chris VanBuskirk Kirk, was the hostess for the two-day stay in Santa Fe, where warm, sunny skies so typical for the Land of Enchantment greeted us.

Kathy Powell
SISTER #4472

I'm from Metropolis, Illinois, the home of Superman. I decided awhile back that I was going to purchase a vintage camper and glamp it up. The journey took over a year. One morning I called my friend Pauline and asked her to go with me to find and buy that camper I had been talking about for so long. Off we went, covering a hundred miles of rural southern Illinois. During the course of that day, I knocked on more doors and jumped over more fences just trying to find someone willing to sell that special trailer—or just one that wasn't falling apart.

Late in the afternoon, tired and hungry, we turned off the country roads and onto Interstate 24 to have supper. When leaving the restaurant, I had a choice of two roads. At the last minute, I decided to take the road to the left. A man had just pulled a camper out of the field and placed a For Sale sign on it. I drove up his driveway and bought my vintage camper. This was about ten years ago, so I had my camper before campers were cool. She is a 1968 Aljo, and her name is Skidrow Chic! The name came from a movie starring Ashley Judd and Morgan Freeman.

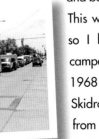

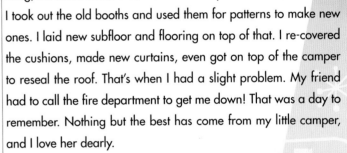

I had her rewired by an electrician, and almost everything else has been done by *moi*. I have grown in so many ways with that little camper. I never thought about not being able to do something, but more about what I could accomplish.

I took out the old booths and used them for patterns to make new ones. I laid new subfloor and flooring on top of that. I re-covered the cushions, made new curtains, even got on top of the camper to reseal the roof. That's when I had a slight problem. My friend had to call the fire department to get me down! That was a day to remember. Nothing but the best has come from my little camper, and I love her dearly.

When I heard about the Route 66 trip, I was one of the first to put my name in the hat without hesitation. It will remain one of the highlights of my life. From Chicago, Illinois, to Santa Monica, California, I met new Sisters and made lifetime friends. I saw so many memorable places and things. I am very proud to say, "I am one of the 'All the Way' girls who got her Kicks on Route 66."

NEW MEXICO

We were even able to wash the Oklahoma mud off the trailers right there in the Santa Fe Skies RV Park at the invitation of Sharon Lambert, Sister #508.

The first stop on the way for most Sisters after leaving Amarillo was Vega, Texas, where the Magnolia Gas Station provided a few photo ops.

Adrian, Texas, was a highlight for all the caravans. Trailers were parked on both sides of the highway while the Sisters had lunch in the

Midpoint Cafe, shopped in the gift shop, and took pictures of the Midpoint signage—an important milestone on day fifteen of this twenty-five-day journey. There were just ten days to go and 1,224 miles until we reached the Santa Monica Pier overlooking the Pacific Ocean. Texas Sister Cindi Mladenka, Sister #3803, celebrated the accomplishment by treating us to homemade sugar cookies in the shape of Texas, dressed up with Texas flag frosting!

Susan Ford-West
SISTER #3580

Traveling Route 66 was an experience that put me in touch with my family roots. Each summer we would make the trip from California to Ohio to visit my parents' family, most of it spent on the Mother Road. It amazed me how many attractions along the way seemed so familiar. I only wished that my parents were both still living so I could have shared the experience with them. My dad, in particular, gifted me with the love of travel.

I have always loved to camp and spend time outdoors. I never knew much about vintage trailers until 2012 when Karen West introduced me to both the world of SOTF as well as living small. I have had the blessing and the challenge of traveling full time

with Karen in the Little Red Diner, our 1960 Shasta home with sixty square feet of living space. Life on the road these last two years has given new meaning to my lifelong desire to live simply.

A member of the Sisters on the Fly since April 2013, I have found such a sense of community and support among the Sisters. Karen and I have attended Meetups all over the country and met wonderful women who have become dear friends and sisters. The Route 66 adventure was an epic journey on so many levels.

Most inspiring was witnessing the Sisters reach out to one another to assist with challenges. Strong, independent, courageous women, who know that we are even stronger when we stand together, are the kind of women I want to be around. And, "we have more fun than anyone" is a motto I can certainly live by. Thank you, Sisters!

Tucumcari, New Mexico, was a blast into the past with motels lining Tucumcari Boulevard, many of which still had their original neon signs and art deco facade intact; some still serve the nostalgic tourists traveling the route. One of the most popular stops for travelers—including the Sisters—was the Blue Swallow Motel, featuring murals depicting this period of Americana on the walls of each unit's carport.

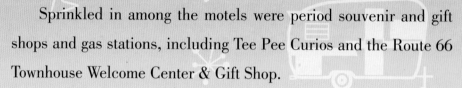

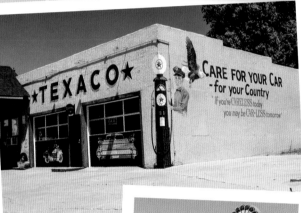

Sprinkled in among the motels were period souvenir and gift shops and gas stations, including Tee Pee Curios and the Route 66 Townhouse Welcome Center & Gift Shop.

By mid-afternoon the Sisters were fortunate enough to find the Blue Hole in Santa Rosa, New Mexico, to take a quick dip in the eighty-one-foot-deep artesian well. Its beautiful blue water, surrounded by sandstone and clusters of manzanita trees on the shore, provided a restful variation from the usual daily traveling routine.

Shortly after Santa Rosa came two options for the journey up the hill to Santa Fe. The pre-1937 route takes the old Santa Fe Trail on New Mexico Highway 84. Route 66 was changed in 1937 to only travel through Albuquerque, bypassing the drive to Santa Fe.

Some Sisters continued on the newer version of the route (now Interstate 40) to Clines Corners, the largest gift shop in New Mexico and strong Route 66 supporters since 1937.

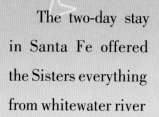

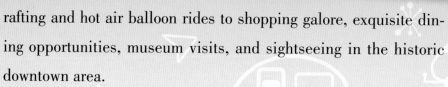

The two-day stay in Santa Fe offered the Sisters everything from whitewater river rafting and hot air balloon rides to shopping galore, exquisite dining opportunities, museum visits, and sightseeing in the historic downtown area.

One of the most interesting repurposing projects of some of the vintage motels on the Mother Road is taking place in the Santa Fe area. A local leasing agent has refurbished several motels to provide affordable housing options in an otherwise high-rent region of the Southwest. His efforts are inspiring, and it's possible to imagine

NEW MEXICO

"I joined in on the fun of Route 66 for the camaraderie and adventure. My boyfriend bought my first trailer for me as a gift. Athira is named after our favorite beach in Thira, Greece, and the goddess Athena. She is my 'happy' place and fulfills my wanderlust and need for adventure with fun people. I look forward to seeing these ladies down the road and fostering our friendships!"—DENNISE REDFORD, SISTER #5143

more of the classic motels being restored to their original condition with the same intention.

The oldest capital city in North America, Santa Fe celebrated its quadricentennial as an incorporated city in 2010. The downtown area reflects this 400-year history in its architecture and the cultural flavor of its restaurants, buildings, cathedral, and museums.

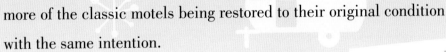

NEW MEXICO

Gallup

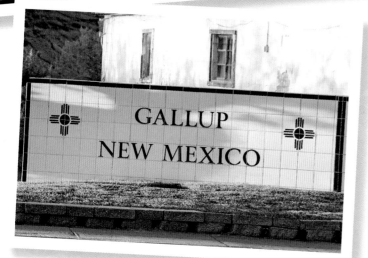

The 199 miles from Santa Fe to Gallup was a quick trip for many of the Sisters because they were eager to get to the Richardson's Trading Company in Gallup before it closed for the day. Its reputation as one of the best shops for authentic Native American art, jewelry, rugs, blankets, antiques, and a dazzling assortment of other collectibles seduced even the most disciplined Sister shopper. It's also a pawn shop, so there were serious bargains to be found—a Sisters dream all in one amazing location.

On the way to Gallup, Albuquerque enticed a few Sisters to take some pictures of America's Mother Road through the now modern downtown district. Many of the neon signs from the historic motels and cafes on the original route remain on what is now Central Avenue. The Mother Road travels through the downtown business district to the University of New Mexico and includes the now trendy Nob Hill area.

From the moment you walk through the door of Richardson's Trading Company you're in for a sensory treat. Displays of painted kachina dolls, bright weavings, feathered headdresses, burnished pots, and relics from a pioneer past stir your imagination. As you make your way down the aisles, the creak of oak floors follows your steps and the scent of sheepskin and old saddles fills your senses. Pause for a moment and take it all in.
—WWW.RICHARDSONSTRADING.COM

Ann Eldridge
SISTER #5566

A friend started talking about trips we could take, and of course Route 66 was on the list. She had already been through the southern portion, and I wanted to see the Heartland. I picked up a 1953 Crown trailer in the Mojave Desert. While I was restoring her, I pondered where I wanted to travel with a sixty-two-year-old trailer! My daughter noticed that Sisters on the Fly were planning to drive Route 66, so I joined and started planning.

My biggest issue was getting to Chicago. There was a good chance I wouldn't make it by the start date if I went on my own. I'm easily distracted, and there are many things to see and do in places like Nebraska, Iowa, and Wyoming. I found the Sister I needed, Sandy Thuet, who was leaving California for Chicago. We met in Reno, Nevada, and caravanned to Chicago, boon-

1953 CANNED HAM

docking the entire way. Sandy was the best traveling companion!

I call my trailer Piggly Wiggly because she's a "Canned Ham" style. She traveled smoothly the entire route. I've always wanted to get to know this country more personally—to see it, go into a cafe and listen to the locals talk, get a feel for the environment—and learn what makes people stay in Tornado Alley!

I had some memorable moments finding treasures on Route 66. In Galena, Kansas, I bought a beautiful 1941 Singer featherweight sewing machine. In Eureka, Missouri, I bought a 1954 Cruiser bicycle and a picture from 1944 of my Dad's aircraft *The Intrepid* at a 50 percent discount. I loved visiting the caves in Missouri and all the little flea markets. Traveling with the Sisters and hearing their stories and adventures was so fun.

NEW MEXICO

Once in Gallup, 154 Sisters doubled up at the USA RV Park. The hostess, Chris VanBuskirk Kirk, Sister #3, arranged for a catered New Mexico enchilada dinner for our one evening in Gallup and a wonderful breakfast burrito in the morning before we headed out for Arizona. Sisters #1 and #2 were along to lead us into Maurrie's home state and a wonderful reception in Winslow, Arizona.

Gallup is an icon of Route 66 history. It was known as the "Gateway to Indian Country." The Navajo Reservation is on the

Sandy Thuet
SISTER #1044

I found out I hated houses—I tried to live in one but was miserable, so when I retired I decided to live in a little trailer. I painted it, as it was an old one, and I thought, "I can't make it look new, so I should make it look funky." Some people in Quartzsite, Arizona, where I spend the winters, told me about Sisters on the Fly, and I looked them up. When I saw that they gave a badge for making a martini, I thought, "That's the group for me!"

I loved how they decorated their little trailers. I like to fish, but it was the camping that really interested me. I now have four trailers that I've rebuilt and a cab-over camper that I call the Wagg Innette since I painted it like a wagon. One of the trailers I call the Wagg Inn.

I went on the Route 66 trip because I wanted to get to know more of the Sisters and see if I like to travel with them.

I do! They are a very fun group and can have a good time even in the rain. I loved the entire trip, but the best part was spending time with and getting to know some of the Sisters. I would not hesitate to go on another trip. It was like herding cats at times, but so much fun.

Janell Farris
SISTER #4980

I went on the Route 66 trip with Kathy Powell and shared her trailer. I became a Sister on the Fly specifically to take this trip.

When I was a child, my family traveled Route 66 from New Mexico to Illinois every year. So many of the sites brought back memories, and some that I thought I would remember turned out to be new discoveries. I loved meeting all the women, hearing their stories, and seeing places many of them had been many times—through their memories.

I am the oldest of five sisters and the daughter of a very active mother. Growing up we always enjoyed outdoor activities, and still do. We often camp together; float the rivers, kayak, or canoe. We all love the water despite Mom never swimming a stroke.

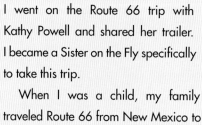

NEW MEXICO

Gallup border to the north and the Zuni Pueblo to the south. Hollywood discovered Gallup as the perfect backdrop for Western movies. Jean Harlow, Mae West, Joan Crawford, Lucille Ball, Jane Fonda, and over 150 others stayed at the El Rancho Hotel during filming. At night even today, the main street in Gallup, Route 66, is awake with neon

signs of the vintage hotels and cafes that still serve the traveling public. Gallup has been described as "Fantastically Funky" by *The Huffington Post*.

The adventure was coming to an end, and although the Sisters were feeling tired, they enthusiastically shared stories of the past nineteen days on the road with the new Sisters who joined the adventure in New Mexico. This brief stop provided some down time to make minor repairs and maintenance checks for crossing the desert into Arizona and California.

"Now that I have time to do things for myself, I bought a new Shasta Airflyte, named Liberty Lodge. Her theme is patriotic western. I just returned from my maiden voyage on the New Mexico and Arizona legs of the Route 66 trip and had the time of my life. I got acquainted with many wonderful Sisters and look forward to more happy adventures in the future."
—DEBBIE RASCH, SISTER #3437

chapter 11

Williams

Sisters #1 and #2, Maurrie and Becky, hitched up early on the morning the Sisters were leaving Gallup, New Mexico, and pulled to the front of the campground to lead the caravan across the Arizona state line.

Shortly after arriving in Arizona, the caravan stopped at the visitor center and entrance to the Painted Desert and Petrified Forest National Park. Petrified Forest is the only national park unit to protect a section of Historic Route 66. Many of the Sisters departed the route here and drove the scenic road through the park, where they saw the highly eroded landscapes, badlands, and petrified wood so unique to this park.

ARIZONA

Returning to the Mother Road, the Sisters were eager to visit the Wigwam Motel in Holbrook, Arizona. The trailers were a perfect addition to the decor already in place on the grounds—vintage cars and trucks from the 1950s. The Sisters readily pulled their rigs in to take photos with the concrete tepees as the backdrop.

While some Sisters lingered to explore the other attractions in Holbrook, such as Joe and Aggie's Restaurant, which is listed in the credits of *Cars* as "The Hottest Food on Route 66," others hurried to the Jackrabbit Trading Post in Joseph City, Arizona. For those traveling the Mother Road, this is a stop not to be missed if you're interested in iconic roadside art and souvenirs. Owned by the same family since 1961, they provide a lovely gift shop and a giant jackrabbit to climb on as a photo op for those who want to wave to their friends back home.

Bob Hall, CEO of the chamber of commerce in Winslow, Arizona, was eagerly awaiting the arrival of the Sisters on the Fly. The Winslow Police Department met Maurrie Sussman, Becky Clarke, and 138 Sisters with their trailers just outside town and provided an escort down Main Street to the visitor center.

We were welcomed with a fully catered lunch, a presentation by Bob Hall, and a walk through town to the "corner," now a public park, made famous by the rock ballad

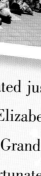

"Take It Easy," where we shopped and then gathered for a group photo as well as individual shots at the spot that put Winslow back on the map.

The grandest hotel in Arizona, La Posada, is located just opposite the famous corner and was the creation of Mary Elizabeth Jane Coulter, the architect of many of the buildings at the Grand Canyon. She considered La Posada her masterpiece, and fortunately the National Trust for Historic Preservation felt the same way when they spearheaded a $12 million renovation in 1960.

Leaving Winslow, the Sisters traveled in small caravans toward the final destination for the day, the Williams Rodeo Grounds. Many of the Sisters made a brief stop at the Meteor Crater, the world's best-preserved meteorite impact site.

The trip continued west through Flagstaff, and eventually the trailers began to pull into their spaces in Williams.

Loretta Lovitt
SISTER #3704

I never heard of SOTF until three years ago. I saw the group on the news. Two weeks later I saw a cute camper at a McDonalds where I met Andrea Ezra from Indiana who explained SOTF. Joining has been the best thing I've ever done. I have met the most wonderful and caring women possible. I finally found my camper in a front yard where it was being used for a storage shed. I circled that house until I got the nerve to knock on the door and ask if they would sell it. A few weeks later I finally bought her. Soon, I realized she was in worse shape than I had expected, full of mold and dry rot and more than I wanted to do by myself. With my brother's help, we gutted the inside, built a new frame and rewired her. Now she is strong, durable, and a pretty little thing! I got to do the fun part— decorate her. I call my brother, Brother. His name is Dean. I named her Miss Brodean, meaning Brother Dean. He loved it. I love him for helping make this possible. When the Route 66 trip came up, I knew this was a once-in-a-lifetime adventure that Miss Brodean and

I had to take. All of the challenges, cities explored, wonderful sisters met, and the experiences have been life changing. I now have the bug—and I don't ever want to stop "having more fun than anyone" with my Sisters on the Fly!

Pam Poindexter
SISTER #3864

When my husband decided he was "done with the whole camping thing," I joined the Camping Divas, a women's camping group here in Spokane. On one of their trips I heard about the Sisters on the Fly, and couldn't get home fast enough to sign up. Route 66 has been on my bucket list forever, and I couldn't believe it when I saw the announcement online. I just sat and stared. There was never a doubt I was going to do it. The trip was an experience I'll never forget on so many levels. I think my

most memorable moment was unplugging my trailer, standing in shin-deep water at 11:00 p.m. in Oklahoma City, to move to higher ground. We visited so many places on this trip that I want to go back to and spend more time. And thank you, Karen West, for teaching me the "two-step turn"!

ARIZONA

Our hostesses in Williams, Elaine Block, Sister #151, Faye Kauffman, Sister #1119, Babs Schmitt, Sister #90, and Jenay Dendy, Sister #131, planned a full two days for the Sisters in Williams, the "Gateway to the Grand Canyon." The mayor, John Moore, hosted us at his downtown restaurant, The Wild West Junction.

We were treated to brisket, chicken, and all the fixins, and dancing to live country-western entertainment.

The second day, Williams merchants greeted the Sisters who were in town shopping with discounts and incentives to take home a remembrance of the Mother Road from their lively little town. Some Sisters visited Bearizona, the local drive-through animal park. Many of the Sisters explored Grand Canyon National Park that day, taking the railway to the park and back to Williams. They rolled into town ready to relax and celebrate the final night of this splendid stay in this western town.

ARIZONA

That evening the Sisters, who usually dress up in cowgirl finery, had the opportunity to get decked out in their '50s and '60s duds, ready to rock and roll and do the twist or hula hoop. The venue was the trendy Twisters 50's Soda Fountain and included a barbecue dinner.

The mayor also joined the party. A live band played, and the Sisters danced the night away to the tunes of our earlier years. Suddenly, halfway through the evening, the Cataract Creek Gang staged a gunfight in front of Twisters, calling on a few Sisters to be part of the show.

It was a great time on our final stretch to the end of the route. Just two more stops, and we would be at our final destination—Santa Monica, California!

"I knew I wanted to take this trip the minute I started reading online about the Sisters doing all of Route 66. I had never been to New Mexico or Arizona, so I signed up immediately. I loved every minute of the trip! I reconnected with dear friends and made some incredible new ones! I have a sweet 2006 Sun Valley named after my mom, Ruby—Ruby's Lady Bug. I'm so thankful to all the hostesses for stepping up to do all the hard work so we could all play!"

—CAROL MCGARITY, SISTER #3884

chapter 12

Kingman

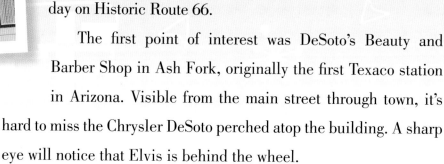

The SOTF caravans pulled out of the Williams Rodeo Grounds with their eyes on Kingman, Arizona. The hostesses and their assistants in Williams served breakfast burritos and coffee to the departing Sisters as they settled in for a full day on Historic Route 66.

The first point of interest was DeSoto's Beauty and Barber Shop in Ash Fork, originally the first Texaco station in Arizona. Visible from the main street through town, it's hard to miss the Chrysler DeSoto perched atop the building. A sharp eye will notice that Elvis is behind the wheel.

Karen loves to photograph trees as part of her usual photographic pursuits, so the suggestion that there was a cottonwood tree growing out of the west end of the Partridge Creek Bridge sounded curious

ARIZONA

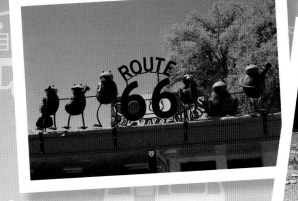

enough to inspire her to deviate a couple of miles from the main route. After all, it was a roadside attraction suggested by the tour guide, making it worthy of the detour. After several miles of dirt road, no appearance of a creek or bridge was found, so she finally gave up, turned around, and fell in line with one of the caravans, landing in Seligman, Arizona, with the rest of the Sisterhood.

Seligman averages around 500 permanent residents and depends on Route 66 tourism as its primary source of revenue. The Sisters fell in love with this town that is both photo feast and queen of the tchotchke trade. Angel and Vilma Delgadillo's Route 66 Gift Shop & Visitor's Center looked like a store from yesteryear—or something seen in the movies.

In fact, Angel Delgadillo, known as the Angel of Route 66, was the inspiration for the Pixar movie *Cars*

PHOTO COURTESY OF SUSAN FORD-WEST

and the establishment of Arizona's Route 66 Association. The other seven states followed with associations of their own. Through the dedication of Angel and the association, this section of Route 66 came back to life after almost permanent closure once the interstate bypassed the small towns along the route. It was good to see how he and his wife, along with other concerned citizens along the Mother Road, garnered enthusiasm for the preservation of these towns and pieces of the past. Gauging from the number of motorcoaches in Seligman, it seems to be a "must see" for those nostalgic about this part of Americana.

One of the most enjoyable and anticipated roadside attractions between Seligman and Kingman is the Burma Shave signs. A true throwback to the original days of heavy travel on the route, these

signs are placed far enough apart to keep travelers young and old interested in the next part of the jingle. Unfortunately DVD players, video games, and hands-free cell phones have replaced this simple amusement today.

Hostess Melissa Kitchen, Sister #1408, greeted the caravan in Kingman, where the mercury had reached 105 degrees. The SOTF Mother Road travelers had grown to such a size that they could no longer be accommodated comfortably at standard RV parks. The Mohave County Fairgrounds—with no hookups—was home for the night. Some Sisters opted for air-conditioned hotels and campgrounds with hookups in order to beat the heat rather than spend a third night without electricity.

"My decision to join and travel with the SOTF was one of the greatest decisions in my life. I wanted to do something challenging. I can now say *I did it!* As Connie Anderson stated, 'It's life changing.' I met Sisters from everywhere, and spent time with them, sharing stories and sometimes sharing tears. I felt proud, seeing other sisters out on the road, knowing that I'm part of this strong Sisterhood. I'm proud of who we are and what we represent, and thankful that these women, are my Sisters!"
—ALICE HEGLAND, SISTER #5711

PHOTO COURTESY OF JANA FURZER

Jana Furzer, Sister #4487, joined the adventure at the Amarillo stop and had to leave in Kingman. On her way home, she hit a big pothole in the road that caused her SUV to lose control and flip both the vehicle and trailer. It was a heartbreaking loss for Jana, but fortunately she escaped with minor injuries. Her husband was able to come and take her home the next day. At the time of this writing, Jana has fully recovered, acquired a new vehicle and trailer, and is on the road again. She received overwhelming love and support from the Sisters, as did all the Sisters who experienced minor and major vehicle and trailer problems along the way.

ARIZONA

Kayo Downey
SISTER #3701

An article about the Sisters on the Fly caught my attention back in 2005, but life was full of other things. Three years ago I signed up, paid my dues, and became Sister #3701. I tented for a while until I bought my trailer.

Driving home from Arizona (snowbirding) in the Durango, Mom kept asking if "Betsy Bobbin" was still behind us, and the name just stuck. It's been such a blessing to meet other ladies who love to do what I love to do. We have great adventures and make great friends. Thank you, SOTF!

"Route 66—what a crazy idea! No!" I said. Then I jumped in with my whole body, soul, and mind and became one of the famed "All the Way" gals.

This trip was the first big drive with my 2014, seventeen-foot Retro White Water trailing behind my Durango. I headed out on May 2, 2015, from Washington State to Illinois. My mind was going crazy and my heart was pounding: "I'm really doing this!" I met up with the Sisters on the Fly on May 12 in Joliet, Illinois, to start this historic Route 66 adventure. Wow, what a trip!

Along the way I made short videos for my mother every day, and the Sisters waved and said "Hi Mom." Thank you, Sisters. It meant so much to her.

ARIZONA

Lyn Hull & Wendy Guernier
SISTER #5107   SISTER ON THE TRY

My sister Lyn Hull and I have traveled on many adventures together over the years. Our story for Route 66 is a bit funny. We read about SOTF in an Australian magazine, *Vintage Caravan Magazine*. Impressed by the article, I told Lyn she should join up, as she is widowed and it would be great for her. I could tag along to see if it would suit me too before we both joined. We happily signed up on the Internet and paid our money, wondering why it was converting to U.S. dollars. We had a great laugh when the membership arrived for Lyn from the United States, and we realized it was an American group. We said, "As if we are ever going to use this." I then humbly apologized to Lyn for wasting her money. Undaunted by our mistake, we thought no more about it.

Lyn then got an e-mail from Leanne Moore, Sister #2011, saying some Sisters were coming to Australia and would we like to join them for dinner in Sydney. This sounded good to us. Lyn said, "If we

do this, we will want to go on the Route 66 trip we have been reading about." I thoroughly agreed with her, thinking this could be an expensive dinner. The rest is history.

We kept throwing the idea around and decided we could find the money to do this trip. We organized everything only four weeks before the trip commenced. Everyone was wonderful, allowing us to join in considering the closing dates had passed. Glenda Stone (G), Sister #62, was amazing in helping us pay our fees. With so many fees to pay to different people and just three weeks before leaving, G paid everyone for us and we reimbursed her. We hired the camper van, organized our airfares, and paid SOTF. We set off on a trip of a lifetime, leaving our friends here bewildered. Many of the men we told were extremely envious—apparently this is a trip most men dream about doing.

We arrived in Chicago, collected our twenty-two-foot motor home, then happily and nervously headed off— driving on the wrong side of the road! We had an amazing time and enjoyed  every part of this trip. We traveled with some wonderful ladies. We admire the passion they have for their beautiful trailers, their ability to tow and handle any repairs as needed, and the friendship they displayed to each other. The organizers did an incredible job, and we envy you girls for having such an amazing group as the Sisters. Once again Lyn and I had to laugh: We spent about $20,000 to get the $60 value out of our membership to SOTF. It was money well spent. Would we do it all over again? *Absolutely!*—Wendy Guernier

ARIZONA

Barstow

Hostess Stacy Edgington, Sister #4611, scheduled a day of adventure for the ninety-eight Sisters camping at the Barstow Calico KOA campground. The 105-degree heat in Kingman, Arizona, followed the caravans into California across the once feared Mojave Desert. In the early days on the Mother Road, the very idea of crossing the desert frightened many a midwestern family who had read John Steinbeck's *The Grapes of Wrath* or whose main impression of the desert came from Western movies.

Barstow was an early transportation hub in the Mojave Desert: first railroads, then Route 66, and finally major interstate highways. During the peak days of passenger railways, the Barstow station was a major stop for the Santa Fe Railroad.

CALIFORNIA

The fourth Harvey House restaurant, established by Fred Harvey, was at this station. Eventually, Mr. Harvey established Harvey House restaurants every 100 miles along the Santa Fe Railroad line. His restaurants were known for excellent service and fine food.

"Ten years ago I left a bad relationship, and my sister Vikki Thurston, Sister #327, lost her husband to cancer (leukemia) the year before. She saw a show about SOTF on the Travel Channel. She joined and shortly after that asked me to come on a trip. The friendships formed on that journey have been healing, powerful, and lasting. I immediately felt welcomed and at home with these women. The Route 66 trip meant I would get to see many Sisters I hadn't seen in some time and many I only know on Facebook. I always feel a bit sad when I leave to head home, as I miss my tribe."
—TAMMY PHILLIPS, SISTER #345

Linda Hutt

SISTER #2095

PHOTO COURTESY OF LINDA HUTT

My quest in life began long before I knew SOTF existed. The fire in me came from a life of working as an RN. It was intensified when taking care of my mother through two bouts of breast cancer: one in 1982 followed by a seventeen-year remission and then her death in 2000. Working in medicine taught me how quickly things can change.

From that experience I became obsessed with seeing and doing it all. I've discovered five principles to motivate me and to live by each day.

- Learn something new • Use it or lose it • Make short- and long-term goals • Share your love • Keep moving

I retired eight years ago and bought a 1969 three-story townhouse. I gutted, rewired, and replumbed it, installed tile and hardwood floors and completely renovated it. Then I flipped it. Now I'm the one who fixes most things around our home.

I am in the middle of a complete frame-off of a 1965 Airstream Caravel restoration and have a 1950 Clipper trailer waiting in the wings!

I loved fly-fishing as a kid in Montana, and joining SOTF brought my Montana roots back to me. Now I fly-fish all the time. I learned to kayak, belonged to a road biking group for almost five years and rode many century rides, and now I'm teaching myself to play the guitar and piano.

SOTF gave me a new love of vintage trailers and a place to exercise my five principles. I found many like-minded friends, and we developed a little saying—"Tic Toc"—a code we use to remind ourselves there is no time like the present.

PHOTO COURTESY OF LINDA HUTT

I found many women in SOTF who had lost someone vital in their life, are suffering with a disease or recovering from one, or need someone to learn from or someone to teach. I found close friends with the same desire to do the things I like to do, with the same fire in life.

I signed on for the Route 66 trip before the ink was even dry because it allowed me to work toward my five principles. I am thankful for the new friends I found, for the spirit in this group of women, and for the reminder of all the parallel things that occur in our lives. We helped one another without knowing that help was given, offered strength and fortitude against all obstacles, and shared our collective wisdom and knowledge. It was a trip that reminded me to notice the green grass, the blue skies, and the gorgeous clouds. I woke up every morning excited to see what the day would bring, listening to giggles, laughter, jokes, teaching, sharing, swearing, and unbelievable support. The words strength, resilience, bravery, adventure, support, and camaraderie describe the trip best for me.

It's all a journey; there is no time like the present! Tic Toc!

CALIFORNIA

"My trailer was named Gettin' My Kicks years ago. She is all decked out in Route 66 stuff. I am starting in Williams, Arizona, and will caravan to Ventura, California. I am hoping to meet as many new Sisters as possible. Only then can I truly say I got my Kicks on Route 66. Party on!"
—PATTI KOPF, SISTER #405

In the beginning Mr. Harvey hired men for his restaurants, but found that men didn't have the qualities he sought to provide the kind of customer service he desired. As a result, he decided to hire women at a time when the only jobs open to women were nurses, domestics, and teachers. A few of the requirements for "Harvey Girls" sound similar to the Sisters on the Fly rules: Sisters rule: no men, Harvey Girls: agree not to marry. Sisters rule: be nice, Harvey Girls: good manners.

The Mother Road to the Golden State initially offered a wild ride through the Black Mountains in Arizona. The first watering hole on the way to Barstow from Kingman is Cool Springs. The cafe and gift shop are still operating, but they stopped pumping gas a few decades ago when the Interstate 40 bypass opened.

CALIFORNIA

A few miles up the road from Cool Springs is Sitgreaves Pass at 3,550 feet. The landscape from the summit leading to Oatman, Arizona, includes a view of the road ahead known as the Crazy Hairpin Curves. The vista is a panorama of three states: Arizona, California, and Nevada.

From here, drivers find a narrow two-lane road with vertical inclines and descents, tight switchbacks, and missing guardrails.

"My trailer's name is Smoochie. My grandkids call her Kisses Smoochies, so it was easy to name her. Every time I say Smoochie it reminds me of my precious grands. This trip is a giant step for me. I have surprised myself that I am actually doing this! My brother Tom died last year, and that motivated me to take this trip. He would be so proud of his 'little sis.' Plus, my sister Karen, Sister #4817, decided to keep me company. We are having some great memory-making times! Our brother is smiling!" —DONNA CLAWSON, SISTER #4440

CALIFORNIA

Vehicles up to forty feet can legally use the road. When towing a travel trailer over thirty feet in length, however, the driver is cautioned to go slow, keep both hands on the wheel, and above all, don't look over the side of the road because it's a long way to the bottom!

Only a few Sisters risked the drive over the mountain. Most preferred to stay on Interstate 40 to Needles, where they unhitched their trailers and drove east to Oatman untethered. Perhaps it was the more cautious approach, but those who opted for the more direct, but terrifying, route on the Mother Road reported that it was thrilling and worth the risk. In the original days of Model T's, most travelers hired drivers to back up the road from west to east. This was necessary because the fuel systems were gravity fed, and the engines would stop running on the steep uphill inclines.

Oatman was a mining town in the 1800s. When the gold was gone and the miners left, they set their burros free. Today the "wild" burros are the town's biggest tourist attraction. They wander through town, poking their heads into open car windows, picking up any litter

Mary Krause

SISTER #2633

Route 66 has fascinated me for a number of years. It starts in a city I have never been to and travels through states I've never set foot in. As a Montana girl, I've spent most of my time in the West. When the SOTF Route 66 trip came up, I already had plans to travel it "someday" with my husband in our 1966 Chevelle convertible that he had been working on for several years. With every new car project, it seemed that our trip would never happen, so the news of the SOTF trip became more interesting and enticing.

Not wanting to commit right away, I began to RSVP to some of the stops—and gradually RSVP'd to all of them, sending minimum deposits. Soon I was all signed up, but still had some doubts about actually going. I had walked the Camino de Santiago in Europe the previous fall, spending six weeks away from home for that adventure. To go off again on a trip this soon seemed a little much, even for a wanderlust spirit like me.

There was a lot of excitement building on the meetup sites. Plans were being made: a visit to the beginning of Route 66 in downtown Chicago, a stick pony parade, a ukulele singalong! For a retired preschool teacher, these plans sounded way too exciting. It seemed a once-in-a-lifetime chance to travel Route 66 in a unique and interesting way.

From beginning to end, I felt a sense of experiencing that "back in time" feeling, of being connected physically and spiritually to those that followed the Mother Road all those years before. The experience of America along the Mother Road, in places that felt uniquely American, brought excitement and adventure to millions of Americans since the 1920s. I was having that same experience now. The drive alone in my RAV4, pulling my red and white T@B trailer, was so enjoyable. I was always in a caravan, my Sisters ahead and behind, all of us having our own experience.

The most wonderful thing, however, was the sense of sisterhood, the camaraderie of women with independent spirits, whose main goal is to have fun with other women. They are willing to pull their own trailers, hitch and gas up, help someone with a mechanical issue, loan a tool, or share a cup of coffee.

If I had one big revelation in my time on the road, it was when we were in California at the end of the trip. All the Sisters were dancing to live music, having so much fun and really "cutting loose." Where else could someone my age go to dance and revel in the night except in this situation, with these loving Sisters on the Fly? Out on the dance floor, I looked around at the beautiful faces of women who felt like sisters and friends, sharing a smile, singing along to the music. Each one of them gave me gifts of sweet memories and lasting friendships. I will never forget this experience. It was unique and special, our SOTF trip on the Mother Road in 2015.

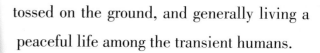

tossed on the ground, and generally living a peaceful life among the transient humans.

Be careful with any plastic bags, however, as the noise of the plastic seems to attract the burros. One Sister reported that a burro snatched and attempted to eat a plastic bag containing pricey jewelry. She was able to rescue it without incident.

In addition to the wild burros, the Oatman Hotel, restaurants, and gift and artisan shops make for a nice visit to this quiet mountain town.

For those who arrived in Barstow early in the day, a trip to Calico Ghost Town was a treat. Calico mined over $20 million between 1881 and the beginning of the twentieth century. When the mines stopped producing silver, the town was abandoned.

Today the town has been restored and welcomes visitors to stroll its boardwalk streets, shop, visit the museum, have a meal, and enjoy the surrounding desert landscapes.

Feeling the pull of the great Pacific and the cool western breezes, most Sisters hitched up early the next morning and were on their way to the end of the route through the Los Angeles basin. They would join 171 more Sisters for the biggest Sisters on the Fly celebration since the beginning of the Sisterhood.

PHOTO COURTESY OF KATHY DOTY

PHOTO COURTESY OF KATHY DOTY

chapter 14

California Dreamin'

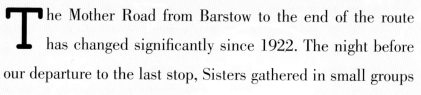

The Mother Road from Barstow to the end of the route has changed significantly since 1922. The night before our departure to the last stop, Sisters gathered in small groups around the campground, studying maps and sharing stories about Los Angeles traffic patterns.

What is the best way to get to Ventura from Barstow? Attempt to stay on the Mother Road the entire way or take the fastest way to the beach and get on the freeway.

The old days of two-lane roads through the orange groves of San Bernardino, the hillsides of Pasadena, the excitement of Hollywood, and the magnetism of the Pacific Ocean are gone. Today it's a voyage on

multilane city streets that can gridlock at any moment. A few brave and determined Sisters, however, did venture down Cajon Pass from Barstow and stayed on the Mother Road through the San Gabriel Valley and into metropolitan Los Angeles.

A few iconic Route 66 attractions can still be found in California, such as the Rancho Santa Ana Botanic Garden in Claremont, the Foothill Drive-In movie theater in Azusa, and the Santa Anita Park racetrack in Arcadia. Most of the Sisters, however, took the fast track and arrived at the Ventura Fairgrounds by midmorning.

Two hundred sixty-nine Sisters on the Fly gathered at the Ventura Fairgrounds for the California Dreamin' stop. It was the end of the road for the Sisters who had completed the entire SOTF Route 66 journey that started twenty-two days earlier in Chicago, Illinois. Through cold rain, tornado warnings, flooded campgrounds, beautiful blue skies, and intense desert heat, thirty adventurous women had

traveled over 2,500 miles to the shores of California. It was a historic and epic adventure! At least another 300 Sisters joined the escapade at various points along the way.

The California Dreamin' committee—Kris Brown, Sister #474, Margo Warner, Sister #593, Kaarin Simpson, Sister #441, Connie Scott, Sister #571, Carol Sacher, Sister #328, and

PHOTO COURTESY OF LAURA TURNER

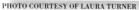

Ventura expert extraordinaire Anita Gunton, Sister #789—put together an over-the-top three-day gathering to celebrate the event in true Sister style.

The enthusiasm grew as the Sisters arrived on the first day. Hugs, laughter, storytelling, and overwhelming joy were the themes of the day as trailers were parked, set up, and glamped to the nines.

That evening, dinner was a huge hit when a red and white In-N-Out Burger eighteen-wheeler pulled into the fairgrounds and began frying up over 300 of their famous burgers. The party was under way. A live band played in the hall, and the Sisters danced the night away.

Playing was at the top of the list the next day and included enjoying the beaches and nearby attractions, shopping at the huge flea market in the fairgrounds parking lot, and simply hanging out with the biggest gathering of Sisters ever.

Dinner that night was a dress-up affair, and that can mean just about anything to the Sisters.

"In 2009, my mom and I found our kindred spirits when we joined SOTF. As soon as we heard that the final stop for the Route 66 adventure would be in Ventura, we knew we had to be part of it. We reunited with our favorite Sisters and met a few new favorites. Mom got to dance with Major Molly, and I got to lead the Ukulele Gals in a concert.

We've had many wonderful experiences with our Sisters over the years. The need to get away from life and retreat to our little trailers is something we all understand. For Christmas 2011, I wanted a trailer, but I decided to be 'practical' and asked for a ukulele instead. My obsession took an interesting turn when I wrote the song, 'Canned Ham Blues.' Now I share it at every Sister event, and I'm amazed at how many ladies tell me it's their story too."
—ROBIN CARAWAY, SISTER #1078

A delicious catered barbecue dinner was enjoyed, followed by dancing to a live band. Beautiful table centerpieces made by talented Sisters added to the decor. Many of them were representative of each Sister's home state, favorite part of the country, or a California Dreamin' theme. Awards by popular ballot were given for the best centerpieces.

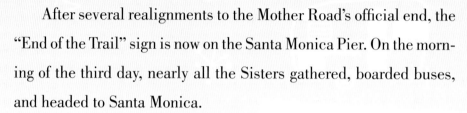

After several realignments to the Mother Road's official end, the "End of the Trail" sign is now on the Santa Monica Pier. On the morning of the third day, nearly all the Sisters gathered, boarded buses, and headed to Santa Monica.

For the "All the Way" Sisters, it was a momentous event.

It was a perfect day that the Sisters spent playing like girls in the warm California sun.

CALIFORNIA

"I had a double mastectomy on March 30, 2015. During my recovery, when I would get sad or a little down, my California Dreamin' trip was one of the 'carrots' that helped me get through it. I met so many amazing women in Ventura! Thank you all for sharing your experiences. The saying below fits every situation, whether it's a Hudson or Chevy breaking down, wrong turns on Route 66, or vicious potholes, tornados, or floods. This is a great group of women. Hope to see you again down the road." —JANET CASTAGNOLA, SISTER #511

"Good friends help you to find important things when you have lost them . . . your smile, your hope, and your courage." —DOE ZANTAMATA

(FROM HAPPINESSINYOURLIFE.COM)

"In 1992, a national event commemorating the sixty-sixth anniversary of Route 66 was held in Flagstaff, Arizona.

I saw a Route 66 skirt made by a famous designer that cost $400, and I thought, I can do better than that. The roadway on my skirt has 'Chicago' and 'Santa Monica' signs, a large star for Flagstaff, Arizona, appliques of classic cars, mileage signs from all points on Route 66, and a series of Burma Shave signs: 'Have Some Fun,' 'Get Your Kicks,' 'The Best Car Club,' 'Is Route 66.'

Ray Benson, the lead singer of Asleep at the Wheel, stopped the show at the anniversary event and said, 'Now, I really need to see that skirt.' He came off stage and signed 'Asleep At The Wheel, on 66, Ray Benson, May 15, 1992'!

James Wilder, of the TV show *Route 66*, signed 'Get your kicks, James Wilder 66' on my skirt, and Al Wyntor, the TNN host of *Video Morning*, signed it too.

I'm glad I saved the skirt all these years. It was exactly what I needed for the end of our Sisters on the Fly Route 66 trip!"—GAIL TEVERE, SISTER #1557

Back at camp that evening, the Sisters enjoyed another wonderful catered meal followed by a ukulele songfest—Hawaiian style—and a performance by the "All the Way" Sisters of their favorite song.

A trip that began with forty-nine adventurous women in Chicago, Illinois ended with 269 jubilant Sisters on the shores of the Pacific. After twenty-five amazing and wonderful days on the Mother Road, hugs and tears and sweet good-byes were shared as each Sister departed, leaving precious memories and dreams of a time never to be forgotten.

Index

Abraham Lincoln Home, 16

Adrian, Texas, 76-77

Albuquerque, New Mexico, 81, 85

Allen's Filling Station, 43

Amarillo Historic Route 66 neighborhood, 70

Amarillo, Texas, 62, 68, 70

Ambler's Texaco Gas Station, 12

Angel and Vilma Delgadillo's Route 66 Gift Shop & Visitor Center, 101-102

Annie's Diner, 48

Ariston Café, 17-18

Barstow, California, 107, 110, 114

Bass Pro Shops, 29, 33, 35

Baxter Springs, Kansas, 39-40

Big Texan Steak Ranch, 68-69

Blue Hole, 80

Blue Swallow Motel, 79

Bob Walmire, 15

Bourbon water tower, 30

Burma Shave signs, 102-103

Cadillac Ranch, 66

Calico Ghost Town, 107, 114-115

Cars (the movie), 4, 51-52, 79

Cataract Creek Gang, 98

Cattleman's Café, 59

Chain of Rocks Bridge, 20, 22, 24

Chicago Route 66 sign, 5

Circle N (Inn) Café, 30

Claremore, Oklahoma, 43-44, 48-50

Clines Corners, New Mexico, 81

Commerce, Oklahoma, 43

Cool Springs, Arizona, 110-111

Cowboy Hall of Fame, 56-57

Cuba Murals, 32

DeSoto's Beauty and Barber Shop, 100

El Rancho Hotel, 87, 89

Fraser, James E., The End of the Trail, 57

Galena, Kansas, 35-37, 39, 46, 86

Gallup, New Mexico, 84-85, 87, 89-90

Gateway Arch, 27

Grand Canyon National Park, 97

Groom, Texas, 65

Harley's Curiosity Shop, 4, 63, 65

Harvey House restaurant, 108, 110

Henry's Rabbit Ranch & Route 66 Emporium, 20-21

Illinois Route 66 Association Hall of Fame & Museum, 15

Jackrabbit Trading Post, 92

Joe and Aggie's Restaurant, 92

Joliet Historical Museum & Route 66 Welcome Center, 7, 9-11

Kansas, 35-37, 39-40, 42

Kingman, Arizona, 100, 102-104

La Posada Hotel, 94

Latte Litchfield Espresso Bar and Creamery, 18

Lincoln Motel, 52

Litchfield, Illinois, 16-18

Litchfield Museum and Route 66 Welcome Center, 17-18

Lou Mitchell's Restaurant, 5-6

Lucille's Service Station, 62-63

Mary Elizabeth Jane Coulter, 94

Mayor John Moore, Williams, Arizona, 96-98

Meadow Gold Milk & Ice Cream sign, 51

Meramec Caverns, 29

Meteor Crater, 94

Midpoint Café, 77

Miller's Standard Oil Station, 1

Missouri Hick Bar-B-Q, 32

Missouri Route 66 State Park Visitor Center, 25-27

National Cowboy and Western Heritage Museum, 56-57

National Gay Rodeo Association. Oklahoma City, Oklahoma, 57-58

National Parks Service Route 66 Corridor Preservation Program, 12-13, 29, 46

National Route 66 Museum, 63

O'Dell, Illinois, 13

Oatman, Arizona, 111-112, 114

Oklahoma City National Memorial & Museum, 57

Oklahoma City, Oklahoma, 51, 55-61

Oklahoma Route 66 Museum, 63

Oklahoma State Fairgrounds, 55, 59-61

Old 66 Family Restaurant, 13

Petrified Forest & Painted Desert National Park, 91

Phillips 66 Station, 52

Pink Elephant Flea Market, 21-22

Ribbon Road – Sidewalk Highway, 43-44, 46-47

Richardson's Trading Company, 84-85

Riverton, Kansas, 39

Rock Café, 51-52

Round Barn, 53

Route 66 Interpretive Museum, 52

Route 66 Townhouse Welcome Center & Gift Shop, 80

Rustic Sisters, 52

Santa Fe, New Mexico, 72-74, 82-83

Santa Monica Pier, 128-129

Seligman, Arizona, 101-103

Sitgreaves Pass, 111

Sky View Drive-In, 18

Skylark Motel, 29

Skyliner Motel, 52

Springfield Route 66 Visitor Center, 35

Springfield, Illinois, 16

Springfield, Missouri, 29, 32-33, 35

St. Louis, Missouri, 24-28

Ted Drewes Frozen Custard, 28

Tee Pee Curios, 80

The Rink, 56

Tow Mater (from the movie Cars), 37

Tucumcari, New Mexico, 79-80

Twisters 50's Soda Fountain, 98

Vega, Texas, 76

Ventura Fairgrounds, 116-127, 130-133

Wagon Wheel Motel, 32-33

Walldog Summer Bash Murals, 15-16

Wigwam Motel, 92

Wild West Junction, 96-98

Will Rogers Highway, 37, 63

Will Rogers Memorial Museum, 45

Williams, Arizona, 91, 94, 96-99

Winslow, Arizona, 93-94

World's Largest Rocking Chair, 32-33

World's Largest Catsup Bottle, 21

World's Largest Totem Pole, 48

Sisters Get Their Kicks

Santa Monica

Kingman

Williams

Winslow

Barstow

Arizona

Gallup

Santa Fe

New Mexico

California